Confederate Military History

of

Kentucky

Kentucky During the Civil War

by

J. Stoddard Johnston

ISBN 1-932157-46-8

eBooksOnDisk.com
P.O Box 30432
Pensacola, Florida 32503

www.ebooksondisk.com

Confederate Military History

of

Kentucky

Kentucky During the Civil War

by

J. Stoddard Johnston

CONTENTS

About the Author

Col. J. Stoddard Johnston, of Louisville, author of the history of Kentucky for this work, is a native of New Orleans, was reared in Kentucky, and educated at Yale college and the Louisville law school. His service during the war as a staff officer with Generals Bragg, Buckner, Breckinridge and Echols, with the army of Tennessee and in the department of East Tennessee, where the Confederate soldiers of Kentucky were mainly engaged, enables him to follow their record through the four years with intelligence and just appreciation. Since the war period Colonel Johnston has held the offices of adjutant-general and secretary of state of Kentucky.

From the original series

Confederate Military History

of

Kentucky

CHAPTER I

THE "DARK AND BLOODY GROUND" — ORIGIN OF THE NAME — BATTLE GROUND OF NORTHERN AND SOUTHERN INDIANS — RECURRENCE OF CONDITIONS IN THE CIVIL WAR — RETURN OF PEACE — IMPORTANCE OF A CORRECT HISTORY OF THE SOUTH IN THE WAR, ESPECIALLY AS TO KENTUCKY — MISCONCEPTION AND MISREPRESENTATION — THE PRINCIPLES INVOLVED IN THE STRUGGLE — MR. JEFFERSON'S VIEWS — ATTITUDE OF OTHER STATESMEN NORTH AND SOUTH — STATE RIGHTS AND NULLIFICATION IN THE NORTH — BLOOD NOT SHED IN VAIN — THE REPUBLIC MORE STABLE BY REASON OF THE SOUTH'S PROTEST IN ARMS

AT the treaty at Watauga, Tenn., in March, 1775, when the Cherokees sold to the Henderson company for ten thousand pounds sterling the greater part of the territory embracing the present State of Kentucky, the chief, Dragging Canoe, said there was a dark cloud over that country. Another version is that he said it was "a dark and bloody ground." The whites, inquiring the meaning of his reference to a cloud, and fearing" it implied an imperfect title, were assured with a stately wave of the hand by the stern chieftain that their title was unquestioned, but that he feared when the purchasers went to take possession the Indians of the north who frequented the land as a hunting ground would shed their blood and resist their occupancy.

Three days after the conclusion of the treaty, the purchasers, preceded by Daniel Boone with a small party, started for their newly acquired possessions, and within ten days the first blood was spilled in verification of the chief's ominous warning. The Indians of the north met them almost at the very threshold, thus inaugurating a bloody war which lasted for twenty years, and gave to the State, which near its close had become a member of the Union, the sobriquet of "the dark and bloody ground." Kentucky holds this title after the lapse of more than a century of statehood. Tradition reaching back beyond Watauga had represented it as an untenanted expanse of forest and grassy plains in which the Indians of the north and south periodically hunted the buffalo, deer and other game, and across which were beaten war paths by which they were wont to make predatory excursions into the territory each of the other.

The aborigines yielded before the march of civilization. The axe of the pioneer felled the forest, and before a century had passed since Boone blazed away for the Transylvania company more than a million souls were dwelling in peace and happiness in the fair land whose natural beauties had been heightened by the skill of the husbandman and the embellishments of modern civilization. For a long season, interrupted only by the call to arms in the national defense, the dark cloud of the Indian legend seemed dispelled and the war path between the North and South obliterated forever. But the fancied security was illusory. In the very sunshine of a peaceful day the cloud suddenly loomed up on the horizon, and spreading with a blinding gloom, enveloped every home with its pall. Kentucky again became in very deed "the dark and bloody ground." The war-path was re-established and legions from the North and from the South threaded the ways which Boone had trod, and crimsoned her soil with their blood. The tragedy was heightened by the fate which arrayed father against son, and brother against brother. There was scacre a home across which the shadow of death did not fall.

A third of a century has passed since this deluge of blood swept the State. Peace has smoothed the wrinkled brow of war. The passions of strife have cooled into the calm reflection of a philosophic retrospect. The discussions born of war have ceased, and the wounds of strife have so far healed as to admit of dispassionate review of the stirring events of that period. A new generation risen since the treaty of peace was written with the sword at Appomattox, has nearly displaced the actors in the great tragedy of the Confederate struggle, and they and the children of those who bared their bosoms to the storm, are eager to learn something more of the causes of this terrible war and of the heroism it evoked than they can find in the distorted publications of the press or the fireside narratives of its survivors.

The history of the great struggle which for four long years shook the continent and made the world stand aghast, has yet to be written. The personal observations of many hundreds of its participants have been printed, and many of the civil and military leaders have prepared volumes of more or less merit; and for many years yet to come these and others to follow will but form the material from the great mass of which, together with the official military records of both sides published by the government, the real history of our civil war will be written. When the actors shall all have passed away, and when to the narratives of actual participants shall succeed the periods of romance and the drama; when all traces of the war shall have disappeared save the imperishable monuments which will attest the valor of victor and vanquished alike; and when the two sections shall be as thoroughly welded into one as the houses of York and Lancaster after years of blood or those of the Stuarts and Hanover—some great mind like that of Gibbon or Macaulay will dispassionately, with the clear perspective of time, collate all this heterogeneous mass of material and give to the world the unbiased truth. The South can well await the verdict of prosperity when the evidence thus sifted of prejudice and free from distortions of error or malice shall be philosophically woven into a narrative where only truth shall have a lodgment. Meantime as the era of the living actors is fast coming to a close, it behooves every one who can contribute, either from his own observation and experience or a careful study of the record, to the accumulation of such material for the use of such an historian and the instruction of the present and coming generations, to put his offering in tangible shape ere it be too late; for "the night cometh when no man can work."

While, therefore, it is a sacred duty both to the living and the dead for all who love truth for its own sake to aid in making up this record upon which posterity must pass, especially is it the duty of the people of the South to marshal the evidence upon which will rest their title to the future respect of the world. It naturally follows that the victor in a civil war has more ample material for history than the defeated side. Its record makes itself, its archives are intact, its muster rolls carefully preserved in State and Federal capitals, while pride and individual ambition secure the preservation of every incident of real or alleged valor which can be claimed as contributing to the result. On the other hand, the defeated in such a struggle, while as jealous of their good name, even in disaster, too often lack the power of preserving their records. Official papers become part of the spoils of war. Fire and pillage, added to authorized deportation, deprive them of the most valuable material, leaving in many instances the personal testimony of actual participants as the only adjunct to the scanty record rescued from a common destruction. In the present instance, the South was, after the war, paralyzed by the maladministration imposed upon the people and, for many years, more concerned as to whether it would have a future than with the preparation of its past history. But now, after having won additional title to the admiration of the world by her heroic struggles toward rehabilitation in peace, and having secured as the result of labor and self-denial a fair measure of thrift, and a restoration to full civil equality, the work of marking the graves of her dead with fitting monuments and collecting into permanent form the record of the deeds of her sons begins to assume a practical phase.

While the duty is enjoined upon the States of the South proper whose autonomy has been preserved as actual members of the Confederacy, it is even more incumbent upon Kentuckians who survive to see that justice is done in history to their comrades, dead and living, who left their homes and all that makes life sweet to obey the dictates of conscience and vindicate their principles as God gave them to see their way. They exchanged luxury for want, the certain rank which awaited most of them for private station, home for exile, peace for war, and life for death itself, rather than turn their weapons against a kindred people struggling to maintain their convictions of right. The war has settled adversely to their views many questions; but while the superficial or ignorant may talk of the enormity of the treason which their advocacy implied, the enlightened student knows that in the first place no court has ever pronounced participation in the late war treason; and in the second, that if treason could be committed without an overt act, secession as a remedy for wrongs committed by the general government against the reserved rights of the States was, before the war, regarded by no means as such a monstrous doctrine as the resort to arms against it has made it. The very essence of the platform upon which Thomas Jefferson was elected, which he inspired, if he did not write, and which was introduced in and passed by the general assembly of Kentucky in 1798, had this initial resolution: "Resolved, That the several States composing the United States of America are not united on the principle of unlimited submission to their general government, but that by compact under the style and title of the Constitution of the United States and by amendments thereto, they constituted a general government for special purposes, delegated to that government certain definite powers, reserving each State for itself the residuary mass of right to their own self-government, and that whensoever the general government assumes undelegated powers its acts are unauthoritative, void and of no force; that to this compact each State acceded as a State and is an integral party; that the government created by this compact was not made the exclusive or final judge of the power delegated to itself, since that would have made discretion and not the Constitution the measure of its powers; but that as in all cases of compact among parties having no common judge, each party has an equal right to judge for itself as well of infractions as of the mode and measure of redress."

For more than fifty years, up to the brink of the war, this resolution was reaffirmed by State legislatures and party conventions as containing the true theory of our government. It had been put forth by men who had taken a leading part in the war of the Revolution and the formation of the Federal Constitution, as embodying the principles upon which separation from Great Britain had taken place and the federative system of government had been founded. But it had a still further significance and object. Within a decade after the formation of the union of the States, dangerous heresies had gained a foothold, and a monarchical element, assuming the theory of a consolidated government, had passed acts such as the alien and sedition laws, and in many ways transcended the limits of the Constitution. By a silent, yet steady and peaceful revolution, our form of government was undergoing a radical change when Mr. Jefferson sounded the note of alarm and, upon the platform of the resolutions of 1798, overthrew the Federal party in 1800 and, in contradistinction to its contention for a strong central government with powers other than those specially delegated to it by the States, established upon a firm basis the opposite and Democratic theory of our government which was maintained for more than half a century. No one dreamed that such principles were treasonable. Mr. Madison, who had been one of the most prominent in framing the Constitution, had used this language, "The States being parties to the compact and in their sovereign capacity, it follows of necessity that there can be no tribunal above their authority to decide in the last resort whether the compact made by them be violated, and consequently that, as parties to it, they must decide in the last resort such questions as may be of sufficient magnitude to require their interpretation." Chief Justice Marshall, who was a Federalist and neither personally nor politically in sympathy with Mr. Jefferson, in rendering a judicial decision in an important case said: "In America the powers of sovereignty are divided between the government of the Union and those of the States. They are each sovereign with respect to the objects committed to the other. If it be true that the Constitution and laws of the land made in pursuance thereof are the supreme law of the land, it is equally true that laws of the United States made not in pursuance thereof cannot be the supreme law of the land." As long as these principles were observed in the administration of the government there was peace. It was not the South alone which maintained them as embodying the correct theory of the Constitution. Other States, both before and after the compact, had contended for them as the conditions under which the Union was formed or was possible. New York, among others, in ratifying the Constitution declared that the powers delegated by her could be resumed whenever perverted to her injury or oppression, and that every power not granted remained with her. Not only was this so, but Massachusetts was the very first to assert her sovereign rights, to the very verge of active hostility to the Federal government and affiliation with Great Britain in the war of 1812.

The Federal laws were nullified by governor and legislature and in 1814, at the darkest period of the war, the legislature declared that "it was as much the duty of the State authorities to watch over the rights reserved, as of the United States to exercise the powers which are delegated, and that States which have no common umpire must be their own judges and execute their own decisions." A mere reference to the Hartford Convention is sufficient to indicate the extent to which these sentiments prevailed in New England.

As time progressed and the profits of the slave trade fell off, and when the Northern slave States had sold their human chattels to the Southern planters, a twofold system of oppression began, the successful execution of which required a relinquishment of such constitutional views and a revival of the Federalism which Mr. Jefferson had overthrown. The protective tariff system was devised as a special process by which one section of the country would build itself up at the expense of the other and grow wealthy under an unequal form of taxation but little short of legalized robbery. The South protested and pleaded against this discrimination, but except in one instance, in the case of South Carolina in 1832, there was never action other than in the form of legislative or party protest, and no overt act of war. The other form of hostility and unconstitutional action on the part of the Northern States against the South was in the nullification of the express provisions of the Constitution of the United States which recognized slavery in three articles and required slaves to be delivered up to their owners when they should escape into another State. This assertion of the "higher law" first took the form of fanatical agitation, and was condemned by such men as Edward Everett, who, in addition to the obligation which the Constitution enjoined, held that "the great relation of servitude in some form or other, with greater or less departure from the theoretic equality of men, is inseparable from our nation. Domestic slavery is not, in my judgment, to be set down as an immoral and irreligious relation. It is a condition of life as well as any other, to be justified by morality, religion and international law." The present generation, after having been drilled into the belief that the late war was a righteous measure to extirpate the horrid crime of slavery, will, as generations yet to come, find it difficult to understand how such a transition of public sentiment could occur in so short a time—from the embodiment of the most cultured and humane thought on the subject as cited above, to the fanaticism which in a few short years has made a saint of John Brown and declared the author of the emancipation proclamation an inspired man. The crusade once begun, grew rapidly from one of mere fanatical zeal and the agitation by voluntary associations and religious organizations, to the deliberate action of State legislatures, fifteen of which nullified the Constitutional provision and the laws passed to enforce the same, by imposing severe penalties upon those who sought to execute the fugitive slave law. In short, it grew from a small germ of sentiment without regard to law to a cruel attempt to incite servile war in Virginia, and finally to a great revolution which brushed aside law, constitutions, and American brotherhood, until a million men were in arms invading the homes and shedding the blood of a people who thought, as all early publicists and the most enlightened later ones maintained, that they were protected against such infraction of right by the very terms of the compact under which they lived. The action of the Southern States, looking to the protection of their constitutional rights from such a tidal wave of fanaticism by the peaceful expedient of withdrawing from the Union and resuming the sovereignty they had surrendered to the Federal government upon well-defined conditions, will not appear so illogical or revolutionary when it is reflected that the tenor of public opinion, as well as judicial decision, was not adverse to belief in such a remedy. They proposed no war upon the government at Washington, nor upon any individual States, and no one had, until after their initial action, claimed that the right of coercion existed as a means of keeping them in the Union. The whole trend of sentiment in the North as well as the South, while many deprecated the wisdom or necessity of the movement, was that it was a question for them to decide as an exercise of a reserved right. In the North this expression, both as to the broad principle laid down by Mr. Jefferson as heretofore recited, and as to their right to decide for themselves, was clear and without ambiguity.

In 1859, at a convention in Cleveland, Ohio, in which Joshua R. Giddings, Senator B. F. Wade, Governor S. P. Chase and ex-Governor Dennison participated, resolutions were adopted using the language and reaffirming the strongest declaration of the Kentucky resolutions of 1798. In 1861 Wendell Phillips said in a speech at New Bedford, Mass., "Here are a series of States girdling the Gulf who think their peculiar institutions require that they should have a separate government. They have a right to decide that question without appealing to you or to me."

Three days after Mr. Lincoln's election Horace Greeley in the New York Tribune said: "If the cotton States shall become satisfied that they can do better out of the Union than in it, we insist on letting them go in peace. The right to secede may still be a revolutionary one, but it exists nevertheless. We must ever resist the right of any State to remain in the Union and nullify or defy the laws thereof. To withdraw from the Union is quite another matter, and whenever a considerable section of the Union shall deliberately resolve to go out, we shall resist all coercive measures designed to keep it in. We hope never to live in a republic whereof one section is pinned to another by bayonets." Quotations of a similar character from sources equally as prominent could be multiplied indefinitely, showing that as far as Northern sentiment was concerned, the Southern States which passed ordinances of secession before the inauguration of Mr. Lincoln had no reason to believe that their action would meet with the result which so soon changed the feeling of acquiescence in their movement, expressed by Mr. Phillips and Mr. Greeley, into a determination to compel them to remain in the Union by force of arms — an illusive dream from which they awoke too late to avert the consequence of their acts.

Justice to the brave men who gave or risked their lives in defense of the South, demands that the truth as they saw and see it shall be stated. No enemy respects a cringing foe, and a manly submission to the results of the war, in the most unreserved sense, does not imply the surrender of mental convictions as to the causes of the war or belief in the truth of the principles for which one fought. The conditions are indeed changed, and the results of the war embodied in the amendments have altered the Constitution so as to make views tenable before the war, incompatible with that instrument as amended. As an example of those changes, it may be noted that every one now is by virtue of the Fourteenth amendment a citizen of the United States, whereas previous to its adoption he was a citizen only by virtue of being first a citizen of the State in which he lived. The latter was the chief ground upon which paramount allegiance was held to be due to the State, whereas one of the revolutionary results of the war is that Federal citizenship is placed on the higher plane. But with this exception and the elimination of slavery, for the maintenance of which the South fought because it was made the particular issue upon which her right to regulate her domestic concerns was assailed, it is a question whether the effect of the war has not been to strengthen instead of to weaken the doctrine of Jefferson as to the relative rights and duties of the State and Federal governments, barring the right of determining "the mode and measure of redress." At no time have the rights of the States been more clearly defined than now, some of the strongest decisions affirming them having been rendered since the war.

Great as was the sacrifice in blood and treasure, in view of the fact that sooner or later the conflict would have come and would have been more serious the longer it was deferred, it is the part of a wise philosophy to look upon the war as not wholly an unmixed evil. It has, in one sense, made the sections better acquainted and given each a better opinion of the other, while it has eliminated slavery, which would have always caused trouble in the body politic and perhaps could never have been removed except by some such desperate process of surgery. Above all, it has insured the peace and existence of the Republic and made firmer the foundations of our liberties and the guarantees of the Constitution. The most enlightened publicists of the world now reject the shallow allegation that the Southern States engaged in war merely to rivet the claims upon the slaves who proved their most faithful servants and recognized that they were making a heroic defense of the principle of community independence and the right to regulate their own domestic affairs, which is inseparable from the idea of true republican and federal liberty. The defense of this lone principle was worth the blood shed for it, and will make future generations count well the cost before either the central power or an aggregation of States undertakes to infringe upon the guaranteed rights of the co-equal States. In its national aspects the heroism evoked by the war is creditable to our martial spirit, while the final rehabilitation of the Union upon the terms of former equality, after the failure of Reconstruction, has taken from the vanquished the sting of defeat. To the nations of the world the spectacle has been a revelation, an encouragement to the oppressed and a warning to the despotic powers, showing as it does the vitality of our system and the ability to cope with any foe in defense of a common cause.

CHAPTER II

ATTITUDE OF KENTUCKY BEFORE AND DURING THE WAR — ITS CLOSE KINDRED AND ALLIANCE WITH THE SOUTH — POLITICAL STATUS BEFORE THE WAR — ITS ACTION WHEN PRESIDENT LINCOLN CALLED FOR TROOPS — GOVERNOR MAGOFFIN'S REFUSAL TO RESPOND UNIVERSALLY ENDORSED — ORIGIN OF THE DOCTRINE OF NEUTRALITY — A UNION PROPOSITION — WHY THE SOUTHERN MEN ACQUIESCED — HOW THEY WERE DECEIVED AND OVERREACHED — EFFORTS OF SOUTHERN RIGHTS PARTY TO PROMOTE INTERNAL PEACE — ACTION OF THE LEGISLATURE — VIOLATION OF NEUTRALITY BY UNION PARTY — SECRET INTRODUCTION OF FEDERAL ARMS AND RECRUITING — WILLIAM NELSON'S ACTIVITY — LAST EFFORTS OF THE SOUTHERN ELEMENT — RESPONSE OF PRESIDENT DAVIS AND PRESIDENT LINCOLN — OCCUPATION OF COLUMBUS BY GENERAL POLK — ACTION OF THE LEGISLATURE — GENERAL ANDERSON TAKES COMMAND — REIGN OF TERROR — FLIGHT OF SOUTHERN LEADERS

HAVING thus briefly glanced at the fundamental causes of the war: first, as indicated by the two opposite contending theories of constitutional construction; and second, as to the immediate occasion of the conflict in the question of slavery, it is proposed to show the part which Kentucky bore in the great struggle. Her attitude, both at the inception and during the progress of the war, has not been fully understood nor described without much error of statement, partly from a misconception of the facts and partly from their being colored by the prejudices or partialities of the writers. The position of Kentucky as a border State placed her in an embarrassing attitude. Allied to the Southern States by similarity of institutions, by close ties of blood, of trade and political sympathy, her people yet too plainly saw the effect of her geographical position in case of war and had too broad a sense of the value of the Union to look with indifference upon the evidences of the gathering storm. There was comparatively little secession sentiment in the State. With all her sympathy for the South, Kentucky hoped to the last that the threatened dissolution of the Union could be averted. Her relations with her neighbor States to the north were cordial. In January, 1860, by invitation of the Ohio legislature, the legislature of Kentucky had visited Columbus as a body and the members of the two bodies had fraternized in the enjoyment of the most unrestrained sociability. In fact, the Ohio river, which was nominally a boundary between separate commonwealths, seemed rather to unite them only the more closely, and no human foresight could have predicted that within a little more than twelve months there would be such altered conditions.

The presidential election of 1860 found the people of Kentucky much divided in political sentiment. The split in the Democratic party at the Charleston convention resulted in two Democratic tickets, and out of a vote in Kentucky of 145,862, Breckinridge and Lane received 52,836, Douglas and Johnson 25,644, while the Constitutional Union ticket of Bell and Everett received 66,016 and Lincoln and Hamlin but 1,366. So that it will be seen that while the Bell and Everett ticket received a plurality of about thirteen thousand votes, the combined vote for the Democratic tickets was nearly as much in excess of that for the former. The small vote for the Republican ticket shows that even if it did not include all who sympathized in the objects of that party, it indicated the slight foothold it had obtained in Kentucky. On the other hand, while the platforms of all three of the other organizations were antagonistic to the Republican position on the slavery question, and while the sentiment of sympathy with the South and its principles was almost unanimous, it is not to be inferred that this extended to an approval of secession as a practical remedy of existing troubles.

In January, 1861, a called session of the general assembly was held to consider the status of affairs, but a proposition to call a convention to decide as to Kentucky's ultimate action was promptly voted down. On the 21st of January a series of resolutions was introduced, declaring first, "that the General Assembly had heard with profound regret of the resolutions of the States of New York, Ohio, Maine and Massachusetts, tendering to the President men and money to be used in coercing sovereign States of the South into the Federal government;" second, requesting the governor of Kentucky to inform the executives of each of said States "that whenever the authorities of those States shall send armed forces to the South for the purpose indicated in said resolutions, the people of Kentucky, uniting with their brethren of the South, will as one man resist the invasion of the soil of the South at all hazards and to the last extremity," The first resolution was adopted unanimously, and the second by a vote of eighty-seven to six. This was unquestionably a fair reflex of the sentiment of Kentucky at this juncture. It was further shown by the action of the joint convention of the Bell and Everett or Constitutional Union party and the Douglas or Union Democratic party, held shortly before this, when the following clause was adopted as part of the platform: "That we deplore the existence of a Union to be held together by the sword, with laws to be enforced by standing armies." A Union State central committee was then appointed, consisting of the following persons, all of whom were the most pronounced and active Union men in the State: John H. Harney, William P. Bullock, Geo. D. Prentice, James Speed, Charles Ripley, William P. Boone, Philip Tompert, Hamilton Pope, Nathaniel Wolfe and Lewis E. Harvie. After the fall of Fort Sumter, Governor Magoffin, in response to the President's call for troops, again voiced the sentiment of Kentucky when he said, "Kentucky will furnish no troops for the wicked purpose of subduing her sister Southern States."

On the 17th of April, two days after the above declaration, Hon. John J. Crittenden, who had just retired from the United States Senate and was the recognized Union leader of Kentucky, made a speech in Lexington in which he approved Governor Magoffin's action, and first of all proclaimed the doctrine of neutrality, to take no part in the impending war except as a mediator between the sections, and to resist aggression of her territory by either section. Upon the next day the Union central committee named above issued an address to the people of Kentucky. After endorsing the response of Governor Magoffin to the call for troops and favoring an armed neutrality, it said, "Whatever the future duty of Kentucky may be, we of course cannot with certainty foresee; but if the enterprise announced in the proclamation of the President should at any time hereafter assume the aspect of a war for the overrunning and subjugation of the seceding States through the full assertion therein of the national jurisdiction by a standing military force, we do not hesitate to say that Kentucky should promptly unsheath her sword in behalf of what will then have become a common cause. Such an event, if it should occur —of which we confess there does not appear to us to be a rational probability—could have but one meaning, a meaning which a people jealous of their liberty would be keen to detect, and which a people worthy of liberty would be prompt and fearless to resist. When Kentucky detects this meaning in the action of the government, she ought, without counting the cost, to take up arms at once against the government. Until she does detect this meaning, she ought to hold herself independent of both sides, and to compel both sides to respect the inviolability."

A large meeting in Louisville, addressed by James Guthrie, ex-secretary of the treasury; Hon. Arch. Dixon, Hon. John Young Brown, and other strong Union men, advocated a similar policy. The Southern Rights men of Kentucky, anxious to avert war, and believing that united action in Kentucky on the lines proposed by the Union men would do so, accepted the terms proposed, and Gen. John C. Breckinridge, just then entered upon his term in the Senate and acknowledged as the Democratic leader, clasped hands with Mr. Crittenden with the assurance of hearty co-operation, and his followers sustained him in his efforts to maintain for Kentucky a position of strict neutrality. Had he declined to adopt the neutrality proposition and insisted upon the State's taking immediate action with the South, there can be no doubt that all opposition would have been overcome and Kentucky would have become an active and integral factor in the Southern Confederacy by formal State action.

But with the most patriotic purpose he yielded to the seductive persuasions of those who proved afterward that their protestations were only a plea for delay, and whose subsequent acts showed that the compact was scarcely sealed before it was broken. It is sickening to recall the duplicity which ensued. Many Southern men, foreseeing the result, yet abiding the pledge, left the State singly or by squads and entered the service of the South instead of maintaining hostile organizations within her limits. Unionists of prominence visited Washington and returned with assurances alleged to have been given by Mr. Lincoln that the neutrality would be respected. The Union press of Kentucky lulled the apprehensions of the people. The Louisville Journal said emphatically that Mr. Lincoln "knows that he cannot have troops from Kentucky to invade the South," and in every form in which assurance could be given, asseveration was made that good faith would be maintained in supporting the policy of an armed neutrality. Yet within thirty days secret emissaries were sent from Washington to organize for the subjugation of the State and to raise recruits for the Federal army. Chief of these was

William Nelson, a native Kentuckian and lieutenant in the navy, whose acquaintance and social standing with the principal Southern leaders insured him unusual facilities for his operations. He mingled freely with them at Frankfort and other points, apparently having no ulterior object, yet was busy arranging for the secret introduction of arms, the issuance of commissions and the distribution of contracts for beef, mules and other supplies. Through his instrumentality five thousand stand of arms were brought into Kentucky as early as the 20th of May, and a camp formed in Garrard county, which became known as Camp Dick Robinson, where in time a number of regiments were organized. This violation of the neutrality of Kentucky, the full extent of which was not, however, known until too late, first awakened the Southern men to a realization of the deception practiced upon them, and produced a mingled feeling of distrust and resentment.

Various expedients were resorted to with a view of staying the tide of war. On the 4th of May an election was held throughout the State for delegates to a Border State convention, when the ticket composed of Union men of prominence was elected without opposition, the Southern sympathizers then having confidence in the sincerity of their opponents and believing that they could be more efficient in securing favorable action. The members elected were as follows: John J. Crittenden, James Guthrie, R. K. Williams, Archie Dixon, Francis M. Bristow, Joshua F. Bell, Charles A. Wickliffe, Geo. W. Dunlap, Charles S. Morehead, James F. Robinson, John B. Huston and Robert Richardson. The convention assembled at Frankfort May 27th, and continued in session until June 3d. Besides the delegates from Kentucky there were four from Missouri, H. A. Gamble, W. A. Hall, John B. Henderson and W. G. Pomeroy; and one from Tennessee. It resulted in an address to the people of the United States and also to the people of Kentucky, in which while the sectional troubles were deplored, and a strong plea made for the preservation of the Union, the refusal of Governor Magoffin to furnish troops to the general government to prosecute the civil war was endorsed, as also the policy of neutrality.

The legislature met in called session May 6th, and appropriated $750,000 to arm the State under the direction of a military board, consisting of the governor, Samuel Gill, Geo. T. Wood, Gen. Peter Dudley and Dr. John B. Peyton, the arms to be distributed equally between the State Guard and such home guards as might be organized for home and local defense exclusively, but providing that neither the arms nor the militia were to be used "against the government of the United States, nor against the Confederate States, unless in protecting our soil against lawless invasion, it being the intention alone that such arms and munitions of war are to be used for the sole defense of the State of Kentucky " On the 16th of May the committee on Federal relations in the House of Representatives, composed of Geo B. Hodge, Curtis F. Burnam, Nat Wolfe, John G. Carlisle, J. B. Lyle, A. F. Gowdy, Richard T. Jacob and Richard A. Buckner, reported the following resolutions:

"Considering the deplorable condition of the country and for which the State of Kentucky is in no way responsible, and looking to the best means of preserving the internal peace and securing the lives, liberty and property of the citizens of the State; therefore,

"Resolved, by the House of Representatives, that this State and the citizens thereof should take no part in the civil war now being waged, except as mediators and friends to the belligerent parties, and that Kentucky should, during the contest, occupy the position of strict neutrality.

"Resolved, that the act of the governor in refusing to furnish troops or military force upon the call of the executive authority of the United States under existing circumstances is approved."

The preamble was adopted by yeas 82, nays none; the first resolution by yeas 69, nays 26, and the second resolution by yeas 89, nays 4. In accordance with this expression and in view of the current reports of the introduction of arms by Nelson and others, Governor Magoffin on the 20th of May issued his proclamation announcing the attitude of Kentucky as that of armed neutrality, "notifying and warning all other States whether separate or united, and especially the United States and the Confederate States, that I solemnly forbid any movement upon the soil of Kentucky, or the occupation of any port, post or place whatever within the lawful boundary and jurisdiction of this State, by any of the forces under the orders of the States aforesaid for any purpose whatever, until authorized by invitation or permission of the legislative and executive authorities of this State previously granted." On the following day resolutions were offered to inquire into the introduction of Federal arms into the State, which excited a spirited debate, but without reaching a vote the session closed on the 24th.

In contemplating the attitude of Kentucky as disclosed by its record, it is difficult for one not an actor in those scenes to comprehend how such a status was possible and how the partisans of the two contending powers then marshaling their forces for battle, while so widely differing in their sympathies and aims, could yet present the appearance of such accord. This is to be explained by the fact that each regarded the neutrality or inaction of Kentucky from its geographical position as advantageous to their respective sides, while a large majority of the people still entertained a hope that the differences between the two sections could be arranged through the mediation of Kentucky. With Kentucky neutral the friends of the South recognized that it gave an advantage to that section greater than any number of troops which she could contribute, since it guarded seven hundred miles of Ohio river front and made of the State a safe frontier in rear of which the armies of the South could organize free from molestation. They also felt an increased security against the ravages of war, granting that each side would act in good faith in maintaining the status quo; since they felt assured that self interest no less than explicit promise would prevent the compact being violated by the Southern armies, and believed that if it were broken by the other side, it would make the State practically a unit in opposition to the North. On the other hand the government at Washington assented to the truce for similar reasons; since it made the Tennessee line instead of the Ohio the limit of the Southern advance, and gave time for organization and for the ultimate occupation of Kentucky when the necessity should arise or the conditions prove favorable. No issue was raised as to either the right of the Federal troops to enter upon Kentucky soil or the duty of the State to obey the mandate of the Federal government.

The paramount power of the central authority as against the exercise of the State's right to determine her own action was not seriously questioned, and the leading Union men who afterward became prominent as civil and military officers enforcing the most arbitrary edicts, had no difficulty in advocating, as indeed they originated, the doctrine of neutrality. It was, in fact, a diplomatic stroke on their part as the only way of arresting the tide which from the beginning set so strongly toward the South. For several months both parties were playing for the advantage. It was a skirmish for position in which the result showed that the Union party won. It assumed at first the special championship of neutrality, alleging that it was the surest guarantee of peace, and operating on the fears or cupidity of those peacefully disposed and alarmed at the danger which war would bring to their property. It was able to carry the special congressional elections June 20, 1861, by electing nine out of ten congressmen; and in August the State election resulted in the choice of a legislature with the same element largely predominating, the Southern Rights men recognizing that they had been outmaneuvered and making a comparatively feeble contest.

Recruiting meantime had been going on by both sides, with but a feeble and technical observance of the policy of neutrality. The Southern recruits had gone to the armies of the Confederacy singly or in small bodies, while a Confederate recruiting station known as Camp Boone was established in Montgomery county, Tenn., just south of the Kentucky line near Clarksville. The Unionists were no less active. Early in July Lovell H. Rousseau formed a camp in Indiana which he named Camp Joe Holt and recruited the Third Kentucky infantry, while at Camp Clay, near Cincinnati, Colonel Guthrie recruited the First, and Maj. W. E. Woodruff the Second Kentucky infantry. In Louisville, under the name of the "Union Club," a secret organization, a force amounting to over one thousand was raised and armed with guns secretly procured from Washington through the agency of Lieut. Wm. Nelson and Joshua F. Speed, an intimate personal friend of Mr. Lincoln. The most efficient Federal force, however, recruited in Kentucky at this time, was organized by Lieutenant Nelson in a quiet way at Camp Dick Robinson in Garrard county, about thirty-five miles south of Lexington. His operations, in fact, were so cautiously effected that it was not until the publication since the war of the official records that their full scope was understood. Hon. Garrett Davis, the most extreme Unionist in Kentucky, later United States senator, was active in co-operating with Nelson in the introduction of arms, but it was not at that time known that he was working directly under the orders of the war department at Washington. In Vol. IV, Rebellion Records, page 251, appears the following letter from the adjutant-general of the army, which fully explains the secret plans of the Federal administration to gain possession of Kentucky:

Adjutant-General's Office,
Washington, D. C, July 1, 1861.

Lieut. Wm. Nelson, U. S. N.,
Cincinnati, Ohio.

Sir:—Your services having been placed at the disposal of the war department for the performance of a special duty, the secretary of war directs me to communicate to you the following instructions: It being the fixed purpose of the general government to maintain the Constitution and execute the laws of the Union and to protect all loyal citizens in their constitutional rights, the secretary directs that you muster into the service of the United States five regiments of infantry and one of cavalry in East Tennessee and one regiment of infantry in West Tennessee, to receive pay when called into active service by this department. You will designate the regimental and company officers, having due respect for the preferences of the regiments and companies, and send their names to this office for commissions. The ordnance bureau will forward to Cincinnati, Ohio, 10,000 stand of arms and accouterments, six pieces of field artillery, two smooth and two rifle bore cannon and two mountain howitzers and ample supplies of ammunition to be carried thence through Kentucky into East Tennessee, in such manner as you may direct, for distribution among the men so mustered into service and organized as Union Home Guards. You will also at the same time muster into the service or designate some suitable person to do so in southeast Kentucky three regiments of infantry, to be commanded and officered in the same manner as herein provided for the Tennessee regiments. All of the regiments aforesaid will be raised for service in East and West Tennessee and adjacent counties in East Kentucky. Blank muster rolls and the usual instructions to mustering officers will be sent to you from this office, and in carrying out this order you are authorized to employ such service and use such means as you may deem expedient and proper for its faithful execution. You will likewise report frequently to this office as you progress with your work.

I am sir, etc.,

L. THOMAS, Adjutant-General.

On the 14th of July, 1861, Nelson in a letter from Cincinnati reported what had been done toward carrying out the foregoing instructions. He said that he had appointed Speed S. Fry, of Danville, to be colonel of the First regiment of infantry in the proposed expedition to Tennessee; Theophilus T. Garrard, of Clay county, colonel of the Second; Thomas E. Bramlette, of Adair county, colonel of the Third; and Frank Wolford, of Casey county to be lieutenant-colonel of the cavalry regiment authorized, reserving the colonelcy for W. J. Landram, who served in a cavalry regiment during the war with Mexico. He stated also that runners had been started in all directions, and that thirty companies of infantry and five of cavalry would soon be raised, and that he would muster in the companies now on duty immediately. Thus it will be seen that almost two months before the alleged violation of the neutrality of Kentucky by the occupation of Columbus by the Confederate forces under General Polk, which was made the pretext of the occupation of the State by the Federal power, the government at Washington had itself in the most formal and direct manner violated the agreement, under circumstances which strongly imply the connivance and concurrence of the very Union leaders who had advocated the doctrine of neutrality and pledged themselves and the State to maintain it.

The Southern Rights men, realizing that they had been overreached, held a private conference in Scott county on Sunday, the 18th day of August, 1861, at the residence of Romulus Payne, Esq., to consider what was to be done under the circumstances. There were present Governor Magoffin and twenty-seven of the leading men of the party from many parts of the State. After full discussion and without any proposals for resistence by force of arms, it was resolved to send commissioners to Washington and Richmond to ascertain whether or not the neutrality of Kentucky would be respected, also to call a convention looking to the preservation of peace in Kentucky, to be held at Frankfort on the 9th of September. In accordance with the recommendation of the conference, within a few days Governor Magoffin appointed George W. Johnson, of Scott county, commissioner to Richmond, and Frank K. Hunt and W. A. Dudley, well-known Union men of Lexington, commissioners to Washington.

The letter borne by Mr. Johnson to President Davis, and the reply of the President here introduced, are to be found in Rebellion Records, Vol. IV, pages 378, 396.

Commonwealth of Kentucky,
Frankfort, Aug.—1861.
[date not given but about the 20th.]

Hon. Jefferson Davis, Richmond, Va.:

Sir: Since the commencement of the unhappy difficulties yet pending in the country the people of Kentucky have indicated a steadfast desire and purpose to maintain a position of strict neutrality between the belligerent parties. They have already striven by their policy to avert from themselves the calamity of war and protect their own soil from the presence of contending armies. Up to this period they have enjoyed comparative tranquillity and entire domestic peace. Recently a military force has been enlisted and quartered by the United States authorities within this State. I have on this day addressed a communication and dispatched commissioners to the President of the United States urging the removal of these troops from the soil of Kentucky and thus exerting myself to carry out the will of the people in the maintenance of a neutral position. The people of this State desire to be free from the presence of the soldiers of either belligerent, and to that end my efforts are now directed.

Although I have no reason to presume that the government of the Confederate States contemplates or have ever purposed any violation of the neutral attitude thus assumed by Kentucky, there seems to be some uneasiness felt among the people of some portions of the State occasioned by the collection of bodies of troops along the Southern frontier. In order to quiet this apprehension and to secure to the people their cherished object of peace, this communication is to represent the facts and elicit an authoritative assurance that the government of the Confederate States will continue to respect and observe the position indicated as assumed by Kentucky.

Very respectfully, your obedient servant,

B. MAGOFFIN.

Richmond, Aug. 28, 1861.

Hon. B. Magoffin, Governor of Kentucky:

Sir: I have received your letter informing me that "since the commencement of the unhappy difficulties yet pending in the country the people of Kentucky have indicated a steadfast desire and purpose to maintain a position of strict neutrality between the belligerent parties." In the same communication you express your desire to elicit "an authoritative assurance that the government of the Confederate States will continue to respect and observe the neutral position of Kentucky."

In reply to your request I lose no time in assuring you that the government of the Confederate States of America neither intends nor desires to disturb the neutrality of Kentucky. The assemblage of troops in Tennessee to which you refer had no other object than to repel the lawless invasion of that State by the forces of the United States, should their government attempt to approach it through Kentucky without respect for its position of neutrality. That such apprehensions were not groundless has been proved by the course of that government in Maryland and Missouri and more recently in Kentucky itself, in which, as you inform me, "a military force has been enlisted and quartered by the United States authorities."

The government of the Confederate States has not only respected most scrupulously the neutrality of Kentucky, but has continued to maintain the friendly relation of trade and intercourse which it has suspended with the people of the United States generally. In view of the history of the past, it can scarcely be necessary to assure your excellency that the government of the Confederate States will continue to respect the neutrality of Kentucky so long as her people will maintain it themselves. But neutrality to be entitled to respect must be strictly maintained between both parties; or if the door be opened on the one side to aggression of one of the belligerent parties upon the other, it ought not to be shut to the assailed when they seek to enter it for purposes of self-defense. I do not, however, for a moment believe that your gallant State will suffer its soil to be used for the purpose of giving an advantage to those who violate its neutrality and disregard its rights over those who respect them both.

In conclusion I tender to your Excellency the assurance of my high consideration and regard, and am, sir,
Very respectfully yours, etc.,

JEFFERSON DAVIS.

The letters which passed between Governor Magoffin and President Lincoln were not similarly published, but the substance of Mr. Lincoln's reply was that the force raised by Lieutenant Nelson consisted exclusively of Kentuckians and was raised at the urgent solicitation of Kentuckians. The President added, "Taking all means to form a judgment, I do not believe it is the popular wish of Kentucky that this force shall be removed beyond her limits, and with this impression I must decline to so remove it."

The result of this effort to save the State from the ravages of war confirmed the worst fears of the Southern men and correspondingly elated the Unionists, who threw off all disguise and advocated the occupation of the State by Federal troops. On the 15th of August, by general orders No. 57, from the adjutant-general's office at Washington, Kentucky and Tennessee had been made to constitute the Department of the Cumberland, and Gen. Robert Anderson was assigned to its command (Rebellion Records, Vol. IV, page 254), and within a short time it became evident that the crisis was near at hand.

The Peace convention called by the Southern Rights leaders was held at Frankfort on the 9th and 10th of September, 1861, but resulted only in the adoption of resolutions deploring the unnatural war, advocating strict neutrality, favoring the dispersing of the Federal camps in the State, and expressing readiness when that was done to assist in enforcing the removal of the Tennesseeans rom our borders. For in the meantime, besides the presence of Nelson's force at Camp Dick Robinson, General Polk had on the 3rd occupied Columbus, and General Grant on the 5th Paducah. The legislature of Kentucky, which also met about this time, directed the governor " to inform those concerned that Kentucky expects the Confederate or Tennessee troops to be withdrawn from her soil unconditionally," and on the 18th formerly requested General Anderson, whom the records show to have exercised that function for several weeks, to take instant command and expel the invaders. Gen. George H. Thomas had on the 10th been assigned to the command of camp Dick Robinson in the following order:

Headquarters Department of the Cumberland,
Louisville, Ky., September 10, 1861.

Special Orders No. 3.

I, Brig-Gen. Geo. H. Thomas having reported for duty, will repair to Camp Dick Robinson, and will assume command of the brigade organized there. Lieutenant Nelson, U. S. Navy, who has done such good service to the cause of the Union by the zeal and untiring energy he has displayed in providing and distributing arms to the Union men of Kentucky and in collecting and organizing troops at Camp Dick Robinson, will accept the thanks of the brigadier-general commanding, who will be pleased to see Lieutenant Nelson and confer with him preference to further action he may be charged with in this department.

By order of Brig.-Gen. Anderson.

C. B. THROCKMORTON, Acting Aide-de-camp.

Lieutenant Nelson within a few weeks was assigned to command in eastern Kentucky as brigadier-general.

It required but one more move to inaugurate war in Kentucky. There had been no act either by the authorities of the State or of the Southern sympathizers which could be construed as an act of war. There had been no recruiting camps within her borders, except those established by Nelson, and while many Kentuckians had entered the service of the Southern Confederacy, there had been a scrupulous abstinence from any act which would violate Kentucky's attitude of neutrality. They were, however, none the less plain-spoken, as shown by the speeches and resolutions of the Peace convention held at the capital on the 9th and 10th of September. Their very forbearance from the commission of overt acts exasperated the Union leaders, who wished a pretext for extreme measures. Having no ground for arrests they began them at any rate, the first victims being ex-Gov. Charles S. Morehead and Col. R. T. Durrett, of Louisville, who, on the night of the 18th of September, 1861, were dragged from their beds and without warrant or charge preferred against them, were carried across the Ohio into Indiana, and thence sent east and imprisoned in Fort Warren, Boston harbor. Next day, under the false pretext that the Southern men were going to seize Lexington, but having really in view the arrest of ex-Vice-President John C. Breckinridge and other prominent Southern men quietly at their homes, Col. Thomas E. Bramlette, with his regiment, then at Camp Dick Robinson, marched for Lexington and took possession of that place at midnight or shortly thereafter. But General Breckinridge had been apprised of this purpose, and early in the evening left for Richmond via Prestonsburg and Pound gap. A number of other prominent Southern men, as Gen. William Preston, George W. Johnson, George B. Hodge, and William E. Simms, left at the same time to avoid arrest on the one hand and the inauguration of civil war at their own thresholds on the other. Thus was the long by-play which had been carried on by and between the Unionists of Kentucky and the Federal authorities for five months terminated in a manner which if it had not been the prelude of so much woe would have been farcical. The hand which had been gloved in velvet was suddenly revealed, mailed in steel and instigated to strike the blow by the spirit of a long pent-up vengeance. The dogs of war were turned loose, making flight or imprisonment the alternative of those who would not bow before the violence thus enthroned.

CHAPTER III

FIRST CONFEDERATE TROOPS FOR THE CONFEDERATE ARMY — CAMP BOONE — GENERAL S. B. BUCKNER — OFFER OF FEDERAL COMMAND DECLINED — GENERAL ALBERT SIDNEY JOHNSTON — ASSIGNMENT TO COMMAND — OCCUPATION OF BOWLING GREEN BY GENERAL BUCKNER — GENERAL ZOLLICOFFER AT CUMBERLAND GAP — GENERAL POLK HOLDS LEFT WING AT COLUMBUS — FEDERAL ADVANCE FROM LOUISVILLE — JOHN H. MORGAN — GENERAL SHERMAN SUCCEEDS GENERAL ANDERSON — HIS VIEWS AS TO LARGE FORCE NEEDED CONDEMNED — REPORT OF ADJUTANT-GENERAL THOMAS ON THE SITUATION — WAR MUST BE CARRIED TO SOUTHERN FIRESIDES — GENERAL SHERMAN SUPERSEDED BY GENERAL BUELL — FIRST ENGAGEMENT IN KENTUCKY — OTHER MOVEMENTS — CONFEDERATE ORGANIZATION AT BOWLING GREEN — KENTUCKY COMMANDS — THEIR HISTORY IN DETAIL

THE first Kentuckians to leave the State for service in the Confederate army were two companies from Louisville, under command of Capts. Ben Anderson and Fred Van Osten. They embarked on a steamer for New Orleans, April 20, 1861. At Columbus they were joined by Capt. Jack Thompson's company, and became the Third Kentucky battalion, under command of Capt. Anderson, who was a graduate of West Point. On the 25th of April a company under Capt. Joseph Desha, from Harrison county, and three companies from Louisville under Capts. John D. Pope, J. B. Harvey and M. Lapielle, left Louisville for Nashville. They numbered about three hundred men. At Nashville they were joined by two companies from southwest Kentucky under Captains Edward Crossland and Brownson, and proceeded to Harper's Ferry. The companies of Captain Pope, who was a veteran of the Mexican war, and Captain Desha, were formed into a battalion of rifle-sharpshooters under Captain Pope, who was made major. The other companies constituted a battalion under Major Blanton Duncan, of Louisville, who had been active in assisting to raise those from that city. They were assigned to the brigade of General Bartow, of Georgia, who was killed at the battle of Bull Run. Pope's and Duncan's battalions are reported in the return of the army of the Shenandoah, Gen. Joseph E. Johnston's division, June 30, 1861. A number of other companies were tendered, but owing to the lack of arms the Confederate government was compelled to decline for the time any more recruits. It was therefore deemed best to establish a camp to which volunteers from Kentucky could be sent for organization and drill until such time as arms and equipment could be furnished. In deference to the neutrality then in operation a location was secured in Tennessee off the line of the Memphis branch of the Louisville and Nashville railroad, just south of the boundary line between Kentucky and Tennessee, and about eight miles from Guthrie, Ky. This recruiting station was named Camp Boone, and here was organized during the summer the nucleus of the famous brigade of infantry known during the war and still designated as "the Orphan Brigade." Col. Phil. Lee, Maj. J. W. Hewett, Col. Robert A. Johnson, Gen. Thomas H. Taylor and Col. William Preston Johnston were among the most active in recruiting companies in Louisville. The first three became officers of the Second regiment, while the last two were made respectively the colonel and lieutenant-colonel of the First regiment, formed of the companies referred to as having gone to Virginia in April, of which regiment Captain Crossland became major. This regiment was the first of any organized body of Kentuckians to see active service, participating in the affair at Dranesville and receiving honorable mention from the commanding general. In the following spring it disbanded by expiration of the term of enlistment, whereupon the men joined Kentucky commands nearer home. The commands enumerated and those subsequently organized were raised by individual Kentuckians, who bore the expense, except as to arms, which were furnished by the Confederate government. Great exaggeration has been indulged in by the charge that the Confederate recruits were composed largely of the organized companies of the Kentucky State Guard and that they took out with them the State's guns. While it may be true that of the large number of men who went South from Kentucky, no record of whom exists, there were many who had been members of the State Guard and a few instances in which a company in whole or part went out with their arms, the number was small and many times overbalanced by the number of Federal guns sent from Washington during the period of neutrality. It was at one time common to charge that Gen. S. B. Buckner who, in May, 1861, when the legislature resolved to put the State in an attitude of defense, had been appointed by the governor inspector-general, had used his official position to induce the State Guard to enter the Confederate service. This charge, however, was wholly false. General Buckner exerted all his energies in good faith to obey the will of the legislature and to preserve the peace and neutrality of the State. To his judicious action and his wise counsel Kentucky owed in great measure its temporary exemption from trouble. By conference with Gen. George B. McClellan, who commanded the department embracing Ohio and western Virginia, Buckner secured his co-operation in maintaining the observance of Kentucky's neutrality. In July he was sent by Governor Magoffin to confer with President Lincoln, and received what he thought ample assurance on the same subject; but later finding out that arms were being introduced and recruits raised within the State while Kentucky was made impotent to enforce her neutrality, he resigned his position, and as a private citizen observed his obligations and duties as such. It was well known to his friends that overtures were made to him by Gen. Winfield Scott, commander-in-chief, to enter the Federal army with rank only second to himself. In the fourth volume of the Rebellion Records, page 255, will be found the following letter from President Lincoln, designed to tempt Buckner into Federal military service:

Executive Mansion, August 17, 1861.

Hon. Secretary of War:

My Dear Sir: Unless there be reason to the contrary not known to me, make out a commission for Simon B. Buckner, of Kentucky, as a brigadier-general of volunteers. It is to be put in the hands of General Anderson and delivered to General Buckner or not at the discretion of General Anderson. Of course this is to be made a secret unless and until the commission is delivered.

Yours truly,

A. LINCOLN.

Such commissions, as well as contracts for beef, mules and other army supplies, were successfully used about this time, but General Buckner was proof against such blandishments. He went to Richmond later, but declined a similar offer of rank pending the neutrality of Kentucky, and did not enter the Confederate service until all hope of staying the war in Kentucky had fled, and the State legislature had invited General Anderson to take command. He then followed the dictates of his conscience rather than interest. The initial operations in Kentucky center so much on General Buckner, and he was so conspicuous in the service during the war that it has been deemed proper for a better understanding of the situation pending hostilities, as well as for General Buckner's vindication, to give the details here narrated.

On the 10th day of September, Albert Sidney Johnston, who had in April preceding, upon hearing of the secession of Texas, resigned his commission in the old army and the command of the department of the Pacific at San Francisco, to offer his sword to the State to which he felt he owed paramount duty—was assigned to command by the Confederate government. He had at the age of nearly sixty years crossed the desert on horseback, a journey of seventeen hundred miles to Austin, Tex., and from there had gone to Richmond. The following is the order of assignment:

Special Orders, No. 149.
Adjutant and Inspector-General's Office,
Richmond, Va., September 10, 1861.

14. Gen. Albert Sidney Johnston, C. S. Army, is assigned to the command of department No. 2, which will hereafter embrace the States of Tennessee, Arkansas and that part of the State of Mississippi west of the New Orleans, Jackson and Great Northern and Central railroad; also the military operations in Kentucky, Missouri, Kansas and the Indian country immediately west of Missouri and Arkansas. He will repair to Memphis, Tenn., and assume command, fixing his headquarters at such point as in his judgment will best secure the purposes of the command.

By command of the Secretary of War.

JOHN WITHERS, Asst. Adj.-Gen.

At that date General Buckner was not in the service, but after the occupation of Columbus, Ky., by General Polk, he had visited that place and endeavored to secure the withdrawal of the Confederate troops. This General Polk declined, alleging numerous instances in which the Federals had violated the neutrality of Kentucky; but agreed to withdraw his forces provided the troops of the Federal government were simultaneously withdrawn, with a mutual guarantee that no part of Kentucky should be occupied in the future. His efforts were futile and events rapidly culminated.

On the 15th of September, General Johnston, having arrived

in Nashville, which he had selected as his headquarters, assumed command of his department. On the same day he notified the President at Richmond that he had appointed General Buckner a brigadier-general subject to approval. General Buckner was assigned to the command of the forces then organizing at Camp Trousdale and Camp Boone, and on the same day directed to concentrate his forces for the occupation of Bowling Green. Accordingly, on the 18th of September, General Buckner took possession of Bowling Green with 4,500 infantry, and sent forward an advance of 500 men to occupy Munfordville, the point at which the Louisville & Nashville railroad crosses Green river. General Zollicoffer having previously been ordered to Cumberland Gap, the line of defense was thus established, with Columbus as the left, Bowling Green the center and Cumberland Gap the right. This was a line which from the topography of the country presented many serious difficulties, there being no direct communication by rail between the center and either wing and no possibility of rapidly concentrating the forces. But in addition to these obstacles the actual number of troops was wholly inadequate. General Polk's command, numbering about 10,000, was confronted by General Grant at Paducah, Cairo, and on the east side of the Mississippi, with a large force, embraced in the Western department commanded by General Fremont; General Buckner, at Bowling Green, had less than 5,000 with a formidable force collecting in his front from Louisville; and General Zollicoffer, at or near Cumberland Gap, had about 5,000 of all arms in a country scant of supplies and with no railroad base nearer than Knoxville. Threatening him was Gen. Geo. H. Thomas with a much larger force, well equipped and composed in great part of men familiar with the country.

On the night of September 17th, the day before General Buckner occupied Bowling Green, General Rousseau had with 2,000 men crossed from Indiana to Louisville, and the next day he moved in the direction of Bowling Green with an equal number of home guards; which body was soon reinforced by other troops, thus increasing the number of Federal arms to a force largely in excess of the Confederate forces and rendering the latter's advance north of Green river wholly impracticable. On the night of September 19th, Colonel Bramlette, with a regiment from Camp Dick Robinson, had as heretofore stated occupied Lexington, while from Cincinnati Federal troops were thrown forward in the same direction and the occupation of Kentucky by the contending armies became complete along the lines indicated.

On the night of the 20th Capt. John H. Morgan, of Lexington, evaded the vigilance of the Federal forces and left that place for the South, with a small body of mounted men which became the nucleus of his celebrated command. He had served in the Mexican war when barely of age, in General Marshall's cavalry regiment, and had come out of it a lieutenant. When the present crisis came, he was quietly engaged as a manufacturer of hemp. For several years previous he had been captain of the Lexington Rifles, an organization which he made conspicuous for fine discipline and drill. He had remained at home trusting to the assurance of peace and exemption from molestation, until the military arrests, of which mention has been made, when he determined to seek security in the Confederate camp at Bowling Green. From the inception of his march his force increased until on his arrival at his place of destination he found himself at the head of nearly two hundred men, most of whom were going there to join other organizations. At first his command was known as Morgan's squadron, but as in course of time it increased in numbers by the accession of daring spirits who were attracted by the novelty of the service, it was in succession the squadron, the regiment, the brigade, and the division. Morgan's arrival at Bowling Green made a valuable accession to the Confederate force assembled there, and from the very start he proved himself of invaluable service in scouting to the front, cutting off detachments and harassing the enemy's lines of communication.

For nearly a month after the occupation of Bowling Green there was but little change in the attitude of the opposing forces, the commanders of each army being busy organizing their forces, increasing their numbers and strengthening their positions. While these operations in their detail belong more properly to the general history of the war, it will be well for a better understanding of after events to glance briefly at some of the leading features which marked this period. General Johnston had been suddenly placed in a command involving great responsibilities and with means altogether inadequate for the service expected of him. His raw troops were ill equipped, while his commissariat and other departments, as ordnance and transportation, had to be organized in the very face of a largely superior enemy.

Comprehending fully the difficult problem before him, he addressed himself at once vigorously toward the work, and lost no opportunity to impress upon the authorities at Richmond the critical position he occupied and the necessity of a larger and better equipped force. Availing himself of the power conferred on him, he sent appeal after appeal to the governors of the States within his department, urging them to send reinforcements, arms and other equipments; but already there had been heavy drafts upon the same sources for the defense of Richmond and other exposed points, and this, together with an exaggerated statement of the forces under his command, resulted in comparatively small accessions. To his other expedients he added the construction of fortifications at Bowling Green, Cumberland Gap and at Forts Donelson and Henry—the latter respectively on the Cumberland and Tennessee rivers, to guard against invasion by water. In the light of the facts disclosed later, it seems strange that he should have remained so long unmolested at Bowling Green when the Federal numbers and resources were so largely in excess of his. But the same exaggerated reports of his strength which lulled the people in his rear into a sense of security had a corresponding effect upon the apprehensions of the Federal authorities, and they became cautious in their movements and were determined to take no risks.

Gen. Robert Anderson, having served the purpose for which he was ordered to Kentucky, in the expectation that being a native he would add strength to the cause, was retained in Federal command but a few weeks, and was superseded by Gen. W. T. Sherman October 8, 1861. There was impatience in the North for an aggressive movement, and the cry of "on to Richmond" was repeated as to Bowling Green, spurring the authorities at Washington and causing already complaints of dilatoriness in Kentucky. But General Sherman, although placed in command in expectation of a more aggressive policy, was at once impressed with the magnitude of the undertaking. He had for some time been on the ground with General Anderson at Louisville, but nominally without command, and was thoroughly informed of the situation. On the very day on which he announced his assumption of command, in response to a letter from Garrett Davis, requesting that troops be sent to a certain locality, he said, with an ominous testiness: "I am forced into the command of this department against my will, and it would take 300,000 men to fill half the calls for troops." (Rebellion Records, Vol. IV, page 297.) He had lived in the South, having but lately resigned as superintendent of the Louisiana State military institute, and knew the spirit of the Southern people and the difficulty of the proposition to invade and hold their territory. He differed from the politicians who thought they could secure Kentucky with government contracts and commissions and that the war would be of short duration. Alarmed at his extravagant expressions on this score Simon Cameron, secretary of war, and Lorenzo Thomas, adjutant-general of the United States, came to Louisville on the 16th of October on a tour of inquiry and inspection. Cameron's first telegram to President Lincoln was as follows: "Matters are in much worse condition than I expected to find them. A large number of troops needed here immediately." There were at that time, as shown by General Thomas' report on page 315 of the volume cited above, thirteen regiments of infantry, one regiment of cavalry and one battery, with another of six pieces expected in two or three days, in camp at Nolin river on the Louisville & Nashville railroad north of Green river; fourteen regiments of infantry and three batteries of artillery at Camp Dick Robinson or acting in conjunction with General Thomas' command, and one Indiana and three or four incomplete Kentucky regiments at Owensboro under Gen. Thomas L. Crittenden. This was exclusive of General Grant's force at and in the vicinity of Paducah.

Adjutant-General Thomas' report of October 21, 1861 (Rebellion Records,Vol.IV, page 313) says: "Left Indianapolis October 16th, for Louisville, Ky., where we arrived at 12:30 p. m. and had an interview with General Sherman, commanding the department of the Cumberland. He gave a gloomy picture of affairs in Kentucky, stating that the young men were generally secessionists and had joined the Confederates, while the Union men, the aged and conservatives, would not enroll themselves to engage in conflict with their relations on the other side. But few regiments could be raised. He said that Buckner was in advance of Green river with a heavy force on the road to Louisville, and an attack might be daily expected, which with his then force he would not be able to resist, but that he would fight them. He, as well as citizens of the State, said that the border States of Kentucky must furnish the troops to drive the rebels from the State. On being asked the question what force he deemed necessary, he promptly replied 200,000 men. This conversation occurred in the presence of Mr. Guthrie and General Wood. The secretary replied that he supposed that the Kentuckians would not in any number take up arms to operate against the rebels, but that he thought that General Sherman overestimated the number and power of the rebel forces; that the government would furnish troops to Kentucky to accomplish the work; that he, the secretary, was tired of this defensive war, and that the troops must assume the offensive and carry the war to the firesides of the enemy; that the season for operations in western Virginia was about over, and that he would take the troops from there and send them to Kentucky; that he begged of General Sherman to assume the offensive and to keep the rebels hereafter on the defensive. The secretary desired that the Cumberland Ford and Gap should be seized and the East Tennessee and Virginia railroad be taken possession of, and the artery that supplied the rebellion cut. Complaint was made of the want of arms, and on the question being asked, 'What became of the arms we sent to Kentucky,' we were informed by General Sherman that they had passed into the hands of the home guards and could not be recovered; that many were already in the hands of the rebels and others refused to surrender those in their possession, alleging the desire to use them in defense of their individual homes if invaded. In the hands of individuals and scattered over the State these arms are lost to the army in Kentucky. Having ascertained that 6,200 arms had arrived from Europe at Philadelphia, 3,000 were ordered to Governor Morton [of Indiana], who promised to place them immediately in the hands of troops for Kentucky; the remaining 3,200 were sent to General Sherman at Louisville. Negley's brigade at Pittsburg, 2,500 strong, two companies of the Nineteenth [regulars] infantry, the Eighth Wisconsin at St. Louis, the Second regiment of Minnesota volunteers at Pittsburg, and two regiments from Wisconsin were then ordered to Kentucky, making in all a reinforcement of about 10,000 men. We left Louisville at 3 o'clock p. m., for Lexington, accompanied by General Sherman and Mr. Guthrie, remained there a few hours and proceeded to Cincinnati, arriving at 8 o'clock p. m. At Lexington also we found that the opinion existed that the young men of Kentucky had joined the rebels; that no large bodies of troops could be raised in Kentucky and that the defense of the State must necessarily devolve upon the free States of the West and Northwest."

The above extract has been given at greater length than it otherwise would for the reason that it is a more graphic picture of the condition of affairs in Kentucky at that time than any pen of to-day can draw. The reader, of whatever sympathies as regards the late war, cannot but wonder what must have been the feelings of Mr. Guthrie and men of his position, who at the beginning declared that they would resist a war of invasion, when within a few months they heard Secretary Cameron declare that they must "carry the war to the firesides of the enemy."

The first engagement which took place in Kentucky, barring a few skirmishes between small bodies of cavalry, occurred on the 21st of October, 1861, when General Zollicoffer attacked the Federals at Camp Wild Cat in the Rockcastle Hills, a strong position, where he lost eleven killed and forty-two wounded. He fell back, but simultaneously the large Federal force retreated in a panic to Lancaster, abandoning much property and spreading dismay throughout central Kentucky. On the 24th of October, Burbridge advanced from Owensboro with a cavalry force to Morgantown and Woodbury, and had a skirmish with a detachment of Col. Wirt Adams' Mississippi cavalry, but fell back promptly. On the 7th of November occurred the battle of Belmont, in Missouri, opposite Columbus, Ky. Early on that day General Grant left Cairo with 3,000 men under convoy of gunboats and landed on the Kentucky side as if about to move on Columbus, but suddenly crossed to the Missouri side and attacked Col. J. C. Tappan, at Belmont. General Polk discovered his movements in time to send reinforcements, and a heavy engagement ensued, with a loss of several hundred on each side. General Grant then withdrew, each side claiming a victory. The Confederate Congress passed resolutions of thanks to Generals Polk, Pillow and Cheatham. In eastern Kentucky, Col. John S. Williams, with a Confederate force consisting of his regiment, the Fifth Kentucky infantry, Shawhan's battalion and other commands in process of organization, amounting to eleven hundred men, was engaged in covering the approach to Virginia then threatened by Federal troops under General Nelson. On the 8th of November, while Colonel Williams was at Piketon, General Nelson advanced, when after a skirmish of his advance guard Williams occupied a mountain defile at Ivy Creek, fifteen miles in advance of Piketon. Next day the enemy advanced in heavy force and dislodged Capt. A. J. May, who with several hundred men, attempted to hold the pass. Colonel Williams in his report gives his casualties as 10 killed and 15 wounded and the enemy's loss at over 300, while General Nelson gives the Confederate loss as 32 killed and his own as 6 killed and 24 wounded. Colonel Williams in his report to General Humphrey Marshall, who on the 1st of November had been assigned to the command of that district, with headquarters at Abingdon, Va., reporting to Gen. A. S. Johnston, speaks of his command as "an unorganized and half armed, barefooted squad."

The Fifth Kentucky infantry was recruited by Colonel afterward Gen. John S. Williams, of Clark county, and organized in October, 1861, with the following officers: John S. Williams, colonel; A. J. May, of Morgan county, lieutenant-colonel; Hiram Hawkins, of Bath, major; William S. Rogers, A. Q. M.; J. H. Burns, A. C. S.; H. Rutherford, surgeon; Basil Duke, assistant surgeon. Its company organization for the first year was very incomplete Until upon General Bragg's campaign into Kentucky, when it was recruited to its full strength and reorganized with Hawkins as colonel, Geo. W. Conner, lieutenant-colonel; and Wm. Mynheir, major. Its company commanders were A. G. Roberts, E. C. Sturz, Thomas J. Henry, A. C. Cope, John C. Calvert, James M. White, Joseph Desha, and W. D. Acton. The regiment served at first in Virginia. In the Chickamauga campaign it was part of the Third brigade of Preston's division and soon after was permanently attached to the "Orphan brigade."

Such was the situation in Kentucky when on the 15th of November, 1861, Gen. D. C. Buell relieved General Sherman of his command. He had been assigned by orders dated November 9, 1861, to the department of the Ohio, consisting of the States of Michigan, Ohio, Indiana, and that portion of Kentucky east of the Cumberland and Tennessee. General Sherman was relieved at his own request, having by his failure to advance and his extravagant estimate of the troops needed brought down upon himself an avalanche of abuse, including the charge of insanity preferred by the Cincinnati Commercial. He had his inning later. Just before being relieved he was actively preparing for the defense of Lexington from an attack which he conceived imminent from General Johnston's forces at Bowling Green. An abstract from the consolidated report of General Sherman's force on November 10, 1861, gives an aggregate present and absent of 49,586. (Rebellion Records, Vol. IV, page 349.)

On the 28th of October, 1861, General Johnston moved his headquarters from Nashville to Bowling Green, and assumed immediate command of what was styled the army corps of Central Kentucky. The organization of his forces then was as follows:

FIRST DIVISION, MAJOR-GENERAL W. J. HARDEE.

Cavalry: Wirt Adams' regiment and Phifer's battalion. Artillery: Swett's, Trigg's, Hubbard's and Byrne's batteries.

First brigade, infantry, Brig.-Gen. T. C. Hindman: Second Arkansas regiment, Lieut.-Col. Bocage; Sixth Arkansas regiment, Col. A. T. Hawthorn; Arkansas battalion, Lieut.-Col. John S. Marmaduke.

Second brigade, infantry, Col. P. R. Cleburne: First Arkansas regiment, Colonel Cleburne; Fifth Arkansas regiment, Col. D. C. Cross; Seventh Mississippi regiment, Col. J. J. Thornton; Tennessee Mountain Rifles, Col. B. J. Hill.

Third brigade, infantry, Col. R. G. Shaver: Seventh Arkansas regiment, Colonel Shaver; Eighth Arkansas regiment, Col. W. R. Patterson; Twenty-fourth Tennessee regiment, Col. R. D. Allison; Ninth Arkansas regiment, Lieut.-Col. S. J. Mason.

SECOND DIVISION, BRIG.-GEN. S. B. BUCKNER.

Cavalry: First Kentucky regiment, Col. Ben Hardin Helm; Tennessee regiment, Maj. J. J. Cox.

Artillery: Lyon's and Porter's batteries.

First brigade, infantry, Col. Roger W. Hanson: Hanson's, Thompson's, Trabue's, Hunt's, Lewis' and Cofer's Kentucky regiments.

Second brigade, infantry, Col. W. E. Baldwin: Fourteenth Mississippi regiment, Colonel Baldwin; Twenty-sixth Tennessee regiment, Colonel Lillard.

Third brigade, infantry, Col. John C. Brown: Third Tennessee regiment, Colonel Brown; Twenty-third Tennessee regiment, Colonel Martin; Eighteenth Tennessee regiment, Colonel Palmer.

RESERVE: Texas regiment cavalry, Col. B. F. Terry; Harper's and Spencer's batteries, artillery; Tennessee regiment, infantry, Colonel Stanton.

The Kentucky brigade is given above as announced in General Johnston's order upon assuming command. At that time the regimental organizations had not been fully completed and numbered as they were later. For the better identification of these commands, of which in the course of this history frequent mention will be made, a brief summary of their organization will be given.

Hanson's regiment, the Second Kentucky, was organized at Camp Boone, July 21, 1861, with J. Morrison Hawes as colonel, a graduate of West Point, who was promoted brigadier-general before active operations began, and was succeeded by Col. Roger W. Hanson, with Robert A. Johnson, of Louisville, as lieutenant-colonel, and James W. Hewett, of the same place, major. Samuel K. Hayes, of Covington, was quartermaster and R. C. Wintersmith, of Elizabethtown, commissary, Dr. B. M. Wible, surgeon, and Rev. Joseph Desha Pickett, chaplain. The captains were, in alphabetical order of companies, James W. Moss, Robert J. Breckinridge, Phil. Lee, L. S. Slayden, Stephen E. Chipley, Hervey McDowell, John S. Hope, Anson Madeira, Gustavus Dedman, and John W. Owings.

The Third regiment, Thompson's, was also organized at Camp Boone shortly after the Second, with the following officers composing the field and staff: Lloyd Tilghman, of Paducah, a graduate of West Point, colonel; Albert P. Thompson, lieutenant-colonel; Ben Anderson, major; Capt. Alfred Boyd, A. Q. M.; Capt. J. Stoddard Byers, A. C. S.; Dr. J. W. Thompson, surgeon. Col. Lloyd Tilghman was appointed brigadier-general before active service began, and Colonel Thompson succeeded to the command of the regiment. We have no list of the company organizations.

The Fourth regiment, Trabue's, was recruited by Col. Robert P. Trabue at Camp Burnett, near Camp Boone, and organized in September with the following officers: Robert P. Trabue, colonel; Andrew R. Hynes, lieutenant-colonel; Thomas B. Monroe, Jr., major; G. P. Theobald, A. Q. M.; Geo. T. Shaw, A. C. S.; and Dr. B. T. Marshall, surgeon. The captains were Joseph P. Nichols, James Ingram, J. M. Fitzhenry, Willis S. Roberts, Benjamin J. Monroe, John A. Adair, John L. Trice, W. P. Bramlette, Thomas W. Thompson.

Hunt's regiment was at first known as the Fifth, but it having been found that Col. John S. Williams had first appropriated that number, it was changed to the Ninth. It was recruited by Col. Thomas H. Hunt, of Louisville, after the occupation of Louisville by the Federals, and went into service with a temporary organization, which was not completed until some time afterward. Its officers became Thomas H. Hunt, colonel; J. W. Caldwell, lieutenant-colonel; J. C. Wickliffe, major; Henry W. Gray, A. Q. M. The captains were, John W. Caldwell, J. C. Wickliffe, William Mitchell, Ben Desha, Geo. A. King, James T. Morehead, Chris Bosche and J. R. Bright.

The Sixth, Lewis' regiment, was raised by Col. Jos. H. Lewis, of Glasgow, Ky., under similar circumstances to the foregoing, at Cave City, and organized as follows: Joseph H. Lewis, colonel; Martin H. Cofer, of Elizabethtown, lieutenant-colonel; Thomas H. Hays, of Hardin county, major; David C. Walker, A. Q. M.; John F. Davis, A. C. S.; R. S. Stevenson, surgeon, and H. H. Kavanagh, Jr., chaplain. The captains were, C. B. McClaskey, Geo. B. Maxson, Isaac Smith, D. E. McKendree, D. P. Barclay, W. W. Bagby, Granville Utterback, W. Lee Harned, Samuel B. Crewdson, John G. Jones.

The command designated as Cofer's regiment in the organization of Hanson's brigade was afterward consolidated with Lewis' regiment, and formed the Sixth regiment, of which Col. M. H. Cofer became second in command.

Lyon's battery, then commanded by Capt. (afterward Gen.) H. B. Lyon, was raised by H. B. Lyon and became Cobb's Kentucky battery. Byrne's battery was recruited by Capt. Ed. P. Byrne, a Kentuckian living in Greenville, Miss., who immediately after the falling of Fort Sumter began its organization. The guns, four 6-pounders and two 12-pounder howitzers, were contributed by citizens of Washington county, Miss., and made in Memphis. Citizens of Louisville aided in the further equipment of the battery, and in July it rendezvoused at Camp Boone and was always known as Byrne's Kentucky battery. Its organization was as follows: Edward P. Byrne, captain; Guignard Scott, first lieutenant; Thomas Hinds, first lieutenant; Bayless P. Shelby, second lieutenant; John Joyes, Jr., second lieutenant; Elias D. Lawrence, first sergeant; Frank Peak, second sergeant. After the battle of Shiloh, where the battery did conspicuous service, Captain Byrne, promoted to major, commanded a battalion of horse artillery with Gen. John H. Morgan. Capt. Robert Cobb, who succeeded to the command of Lyon's battery, was from Lyon county, Ky., and the battery, known afterward by his name, was in constant service to the close of the war. Its officers were Frank P. Gracey, first lieutenant; Barclay A. James, second lieutenant; I. R. Dudley, first sergeant, and W. E. Etheridge, second sergeant. Spencer's battery of the reserve, in December strengthened by recruits from the five Kentucky regiments, became Graves' battery, under command of Capt. Rice E. Graves, a West Point cadet from Kentucky, who distinguished himself and fell on the second day at Murfreesboro. To the commands enumerated above must be added Morgan's cavalry squadron, and the Eighth Kentucky infantry, commanded by Col. H. B. Lyon, which completes the list of Kentucky organizations then in the field.

CHAPTER IV

POLITICAL MOVEMENTS — GENERAL JOHN C. BRECKINRIDGE RESIGNS HIS SEAT AS U. S. SENATOR — ENTERS CONFEDERATE ARMY AT BOWLING GREEN — ORGANIZATION OF PROVISIONAL GOVERNMENT AT RUSSELLVILLE — GEORGE W. JOHNSON CHOSEN — CONFEDERATE DEFEAT AT FISHING CREEK, CALLED BY FEDERALS BATTLE OF MILL SPRINGS — A SERIOUS DISASTER — DEATH OF GENERAL ZOLLICOFFER — GENERAL GEORGE B. CRITTENDEN — CRITICAL POSITION OF GENERAL JOHNSTON AT BOWLING GREEN — FALL OF FORT HENRY — GENERALS FLOYD AND BUCKNER SENT WITH THEIR DIVISIONS TO DEFEND FORT DONELSON

BEFORE entering upon an account of the military operations which eventuated in the evacuation of Kentucky, it will be well to note briefly the political movements at this period. When the reign of terror was inaugurated in central Kentucky by the arrest of Southern men and their transportation to Northern prisons, a large number of leading Kentuckians, including some members of the legislature, sought safety in the Confederate lines, and most of them entered the army. Senator Breckinridge, upon his arrival in Bowling Green on the 8th of October, issued an address to the people of Kentucky, in which he reviewed the events of the past year and exposed the duplicity and usurpation which had placed Kentucky in the deplorable condition she then was, and closed by resigning his seat in the United States Senate. "To defend your birthright and mine," said he, "which is more precious than domestic ease or property or life, I exchange with proud satisfaction a term of six years in the Senate of the United States for the musket of a soldier." How fully he vindicated his title to the honors with which Kentucky had wreathed his young brow, is shown in a military record as brilliant as that of his civil life; and how gratefully Kentucky recognized his sacrifices in her behalf is attested by the statue in imperishable bronze erected at Lexington a quarter of a century from that time, by the legislature of the State and his admiring fellow citizens.

On the 18th of November, 1861, a convention was held at Russellville, Ky., composed of delegates from the counties within the Confederate lines, and of refugees from many other counties within the Federal lines, comprising over two hundred members representing sixty-five counties. It was in session three days and adopted an ordinance of secession and a provisional form of State government. George W. Johnson, of Scott county, was chosen governor, and other executive officers named. Henry C. Burnett, Wm. E. Simms and William Preston were sent to Richmond as commissioners to negotiate an alliance with the Confederates, and as the result the Congress of the Confederate States admitted the State as a member of the Confederacy on the 10th of December, 1861. Two senators and twelve members of Congress were then elected provisionally by the executive council, and during the war a congressional ticket was elected biennially by the soldiers from Kentucky.* On the 14th of November Senator Breckinridge, who had been meantime commissioned brigadier-general, was assigned to the command of the Kentucky brigade, Buckner's division, and on the 16th he assumed command, with the following staff: Capt. Geo. B. Hodge, A. A. G.; Maj. Alfred Boyd, A. Q. M.; Capt. Clint McCarty, A. C. S.; and Capt. T. T. Hawkins, A. D. C.

With the accession of General Buell to the Federal command came a change of policy, looking to the shortening of lines and the greater concentration of troops in the direction of Bowling Green. General Thomas, who had been operating toward Cumberland Gap, was moved to Somerset and also occupied points on the upper Green river upon General Johnston's right flank. Preparations were also made for an advance upon the latter's front by repairing the Green river bridge at Munfordville. The condition of the roads on the Cumberland Gap line rendering movements there by either army impracticable, General Zollicoffer's command was transferred to Monticello, placing him in closer connection with General Johnston and looking to the better protection of the right flank. His force was also increased, and Maj.-Gen. Geo. B. Crittenden assigned to its command. Evidences of increased Federal activity were shown on General Johnston's left. The Tennessee and Cumberland rivers, which had been low, were made navigable for gunboats by the early winter rains; and General Johnston, who early foresaw the danger of having his line penetrated by a movement in force up those rivers, thus threatening Nashville and passing between

*For the Provisional government, with members of Congress, see Appendix A.

him and General Polk, took every precaution to guard against such result. The best engineers had been sent to the narrow strip which separates these two rivers just south of the Tennessee and Kentucky line, and fortifications erected at Fort Henry on the Tennessee and Fort Donelson on the Cumberland rivers. Similar fortifications had been made at Clarksville, Tenn., to which place Gen. Lloyd Tilghman, who had been stationed with a force of observation at Hopkinsville, was assigned. Subsequently he was placed in charge of Fort Henry.

But a serious disaster occurred on General Johnston's right flank in the defeat of General Crittenden at Fishing Creek, Pulaski county, Ky., on the 19th of January, 1862. Mill Springs is a small hamlet on the south side of the Cumberland river just above which Fishing Creek, which flows from the north, empties into the Cumberland. On the 17th General Crittenden was occupying Mill Springs with the Seventeenth, Twenty-eighth and Thirty-seventh Tennessee regiments, the First battalion Tennessee cavalry, two companies of the Third battalion Tennessee cavalry and four pieces of artillery. At the same time he had at Beech Grove, directly opposite, on the north side of the river, the Fifteenth Mississippi, Sixteenth Alabama, Nineteenth, Twentieth, Twenty-fifth and Twenty-ninth Tennessee regiments, two battalions of Tennessee cavalry, two independent cavalry companies and twelve pieces of artillery, a total of about 4,000 men. For some time the army of General Thomas had occupied Somerset, 18 miles north-easterly, with eight regiments of infantry, and Columbia, 35 miles to the northwest, with five regiments of infantry. Having learned on the 18th that the Columbia force was camped at Logan's Cross Roads, ten miles north of Beech Grove, in expectation of effecting a junction with the omerset force, and that this would be retarded by the high stage of water in the creek, he determined to attack before the junction could be effected. He therefore united his forces on the north side, and at midnight on the 18th having previously learned that the enemy was advancing, he moved against him. His force of two brigades, commanded by Gen. F. K. Zollicoffer and Gen. W. H. Carroll, marched northward on the road leading to Logan's Cross Roads and at daylight the cavalry advance came in contact with the enemy's pickets. A line of battle being formed, the skirmishers were soon engaged. The enemy was not taken by surprise as was hoped, and besides his forces had effected the junction. Rain was falling, and the morning was so dark that General Zollicoffer, mistaking a Federal regiment for one of his own, rode into it and was killed, as General Crittenden states, "within bayonet reach," by the pistol shot of a Federal officer. This had a dispiriting effect on the Confederate forces, and although they behaved with gallantry for several hours against a greatly superior force, they finally retreated to their camp on the Cumberland pursued by the enemy, but not attacked after reaching Beech Grove. During the night General Crittenden crossed his army to the south side, but with the loss of his artillery, wagons and animals, stores, ammunition, etc. He retreated in a demoralized condition to Gainesboro, Tenn., eighty miles lower down on the Cumberland. In his report (Rebellion Records, Vol. VII, page 205), he states his loss at 126 killed, 309 wounded and 95 missing, and estimates the Federal loss at 700, while General Thomas in his report estimates the Confederate force at 12,000, and states his own loss at 39 killed and 207 wounded.

Under all the circumstances the death of General Zollicoffer and the disaster of Fishing Creek came as a severe blow to the Confederates. It greatly cheered the Federalists in Kentucky and cast a gloom over the opposite side. Its strategic effect was of the most serious character, as it wholly uncovered General Johnston's right flank and rendered his advanced position at Bowling Green still more critical. General Buell's plan from the start was to menace him in front until he could dislodge him by a flank movement. He had no idea of moving on him in his intrenched position and putting Green river at his back. He had great difficulty in resisting importunities from Washington to push Thomas into East Tennessee through Cumberland Gap, and adhered to his own plan in his operations, which resulted in the defeat of Crittenden. Mr. Lincoln, barring his eagerness to please Brownlow and Andrew Johnson, in a letter to General Buell of January 13, 1862 (Rebellion Records, Vol. VII, page 929), expresses in his homely way a comprehension of the true strategy: "My idea is that Halleck shall menace Columbus and 'down-river' generally, while you menace Bowling Green and East Tennessee. If the enemy shall concentrate at Bowling Green, do not retire from his front, yet do not fight him there either, but seize Columbus and East Tennessee, one or both, left exposed by the concentration at Bowling Green. It is a matter of no small anxiety to me, and which I am sure you will not overlook, that the

East Tennessee line is so long and over so bad a road." Buell was not a politician, and from a military standpoint never regarded the occupation of East Tennessee as a paramount necessity. His failure to pander to this sentiment was an important factor in his ultimate downfall, as we shall see in time.

With the success of General Thomas on the right flank of the Confederate army of occupation, evidences of a formidable movement on the left soon became apparent. On the 6th of February a heavy attack was made upon Fort Henry by a gunboat expedition, and after a bombardment in which the Confederate batteries were greatly damaged, Gen. Lloyd Tilghman was forced to surrender after a gallant defense, with eighty men, his infantry numbering nearly 3,000 men, under Colonel Heiman, falling back on Fort Donelson. To the defense of this position, the attack on which now became imminent, General Johnston sent General Pillow with his command of 4,000 on the 9th of February, and on the 12th reinforced him with the commands of Generals Floyd and Buckner, 8,000 more, making the garrison force in the aggregate nominally 15,000 men, but really several thousand less, excluding sick left behind. At the same time recognizing the danger to which he would be exposed at Bowling Green by the depletion of his force and the necessity of covering Nashville, he began the evacuation of the former place on the evening of the 11th, General Buell reaching Bowling Green on the evening of the 12th and General Johnston's army being in front of Nashville on the 15th, the withdrawal being made without loss of any material and in perfect order.

CHAPTER V

SITUATION AT FORT DONELSON — DISPOSITION OF FORCES — ACCOUNT OF THE BATTLE — ATTACK BY THE GUNBOATS — THEIR REPULSE — GENERAL GRANT INVESTS CONFEDERATE LINES — SORTIE IN FORCE BY THE CONFEDERATES — ITS SUCCESS — BLOODY REPULSE OF THE FEDERALS — ESCAPE OF CONFEDERATE ARMY INSURED WHEN THE TROOPS WERE ORDERED BACK INTO THE TRENCHES — INDEFENSIBLE POSITION — SEVERE WEATHER — EXPOSURE AND SUFFERING OF CONFEDERATE TROOPS — GALLANT FIGHTING OF COLONEL HARRISON AND SECOND KENTUCKY, AND COLONEL LYON AND EIGHTH KENTUCKY — COUNCIL OF WAR — GENERALS FLOYD AND PILLOW TURN THE COMMAND OVER TO GENERAL BUCKNER AND ESCAPE TO NASHVILLE — GENERAL BUCKNER SURRENDERS TO GENERAL GRANT

THE fall of Fort Donelson which occurred on February 16, 1862, was a far-reaching disaster, which opened up to the occupation by the enemy not only all of Kentucky, but all of Tennessee west of the Cumberland mountains. As the details of the battle belong properly to the history of the Confederate operations in Tennessee, only such reference to them will be made as is necessary to show the part taken by the Kentucky troops. General Pillow being in command at Fort Donelson, and an attack being imminent, the commands of Generals Buckner and Floyd, which had for several days been at Clarksville, were moved by boat, and the last of them arrived with General Floyd on the night of the 12th. General Buckner, in his report (Rebellion Records, Vol. VII, page 329), says: "The defenses were in a very imperfect condition. The space to be defended by the army was quadrangular in shape, being limited on the north by the Cumberland river, on the east and west by small streams now converted into deep sloughs by the high water, and on the south by our line of defense. The river line exceeded a mile in length. The line of defense was about two miles and a half long, and its distance from the river varied from one-fourth to three-fourths of a mile. The line of intrenchments consisted of a few logs rolled together and but slightly covered with earth, forming an insufficient protection even against field artillery. Not more than one-third of the line was completed on the morning of the 12th. * * * Work on my lines was prosecuted with energy and was urged forward as rapidly as the limited number of tools would permit, so that by the morning of the 13th my position was in a respectable state of defense."

General Buckner was placed in command of the right wing, and Gen. Bushrod R. Johnson of the left. The only Kentucky troops present were the Second regiment under Col. Roger W. Hanson, Graves' battery, and the Eighth Kentucky regiment, Lieut.-Col. H. B. Lyon. The first two were on the extreme right of General Buckner's line, while the last was near the left of General Johnson's line, attached to the brigade of Col. John M. Simonton, of Mississippi.

General Grant, who had with his army ascended the Tennessee river and landed at Fort Henry, ten miles westward, on the morning of the 12th, marched with 15,000 men, comprising the divisions of Generals John A. McClernand and C. F. Smith, and at noon arrived within two miles of Fort Donelson and drove in the Confederate pickets. Had he moved on the works at once with this large force, their capture would have been comparatively easy, as many of Floyd's command had not arrived, and the Confederates were ill prepared for an attack. He had, however, sent six regiments from Fort Henry around by water convoyed by a gunboat, and, awaiting their arrival, his plan was not to make a general attack but to invest the works as closely as he could with safety. (See his report on page 159 of the volume quoted above, in which the reports of officers of both armies will be found.) "About ten o'clock on the morning of the 13th," General Buckner says, "the enemy made a vigorous attack on Hanson's position, but was repelled with heavy loss. The attack was subsequently renewed by three heavy regiments, but was again repulsed by the Second Kentucky regiment, aided by a part of the Eighteenth Tennessee, Col. J. B. Palmer." The Confederate troops remained in their trenches and their loss was small, although throughout the day the fire along the line was incessant and kept up through the night.

On the 14th, the gunboats having arrived the night before, there was no land attack; but at two o'clock a heavy bombardment was begun by six gunboats under Admiral Foote and continued two hours when, having been disabled by the Confederate water batteries, they withdrew without having inflicted any damage to the batteries or killed a man. It was then General

Grant's purpose to repair the gunboats before assaulting the Confederate lines, which were now completely invested, his force having been augmented by the arrival of Gen. Lew Wallace's division, about 7,000 strong, from Fort Henry. The disposition of his army was as follows: McClernand's division on the right, Wallace's in the center and Smith's on the left. Meantime the weather had, on the 13th, turned very cold, with snow and rain which bore heavily upon the Confederate troops exposed in the trenches and already worn down by incessant duty for three days and nights.

It became evident to the Confederate commanders that to remain inactive rendered capture a question of but a short time, as retreat was cut off by the extension of both the enemy's wings to the river. A council being held on the night of the 14th, it was decided that the only alternative was to drive back the enemy's right wing by an early attack in the morning, and having cleared the way, to retreat in the direction of Nashville by the way of Charlotte. Accordingly, on the morning of Saturday, the 15th, at five o'clock, the attack was made on General Grant's right, and the enemy being pressed back after a time in disorder, General Buckner also advanced and the movement was kept up until victory seemed complete, the Federal right having been driven several miles, while General Buckner had driven his left so far as to uncover the proposed route of retreat, and the object of the battle seemed safely accomplished. At this juncture, when General Buckner was two miles from his works and expecting the retreat to begin, he received orders from General Pillow to return to the intrenchments.

It is useless to prolong the painful narrative. The whole army returned to their cheerless trenches worn down with fatigue and depressed with the failure to be extricated from the hopeless position which their intelligence told them they now occupied. Added to this, the enemy being further reinforced, and learning of the withdrawal of the Confederates within their lines, followed them up vigorously and before dark had resumed the investment and also effected a lodgment at the extreme right of our line. The rest is known, how at a council of war, the desperate condition having been recognized, a surrender was deemed the only course left; how the senior commanders in turn declined to carry out the decision and, turning the command over to General Buckner, left him to share the fate of his men, while they effected their escape by boat with a small force, before negotiations set in; and how at daylight a bugler and a flag terminated further contest. Let us draw the curtain on the sad event, the intelligence of which carried such woe to the whole South and to their friends in Kentucky who shared all their joys and sorrows, and who in their own good time testified their admiration of true heroism by electing as governor, with the hearty concurrence of many of the Federal soldiers, the gallant Buckner, who was the chief prisoner of this surrender. Far be it from the purpose of the writer to reflect upon the courage or patriotism of Generals Floyd and Pillow. It was a question for each to decide for himself, and if they erred in judgment, most grievous must have been their suffering.

General Buckner in his report speaks in terms of the highest praise of Colonel Hanson and his regiment, and of Graves' battery. Speaking of one point in the action of the 15th, an advance upon the right ordered by him at a critical time, he says: "In this latter movement a section of Graves' battery participated, playing with destructive effect upon the enemy's left, while about the same time the Second Kentucky, under Colonel Hanson, charged in quick time as if upon parade, through an open field and under a destructive fire, without firing a gun, upon a superior force of the enemy, who broke and fled in all directions. A large portion of the enemy's right dispersed through the woods and made their way, as was afterward learned, to Fort Henry."

Colonel Hanson, in referring to the same incident in his report, says: "In front of us was an open space which had formerly been occupied as a camp. This space was about two hundred yards in width. Beyond the space in the timber and thick undergrowth the enemy were posted. I directed the regiment, when the command was given, to march at quick time across the space and not to fire a gun until they reached the woods in which the enemy were posted. The order was admirably executed, and although we lost 50 men in killed and wounded in crossing the space, not a gun was fired until the woods were reached. The enemy stood their ground until we were within 40 yards of them, when they fled in great confusion under a most destructive fire. This was not strictly speaking a 'charge bayonets,' but it would have been if the enemy had not fled."

The staff of General Buckner shared his fortunes. In his report he says: "Maj. Geo. B. Cosby, my chief of staff, deserves the highest commendation for the gallant and intelligent discharge of his duties, and the other members of my staff are entitled to my thanks for their gallantry and the efficient discharge of their appropriate duties. Lieutenants Charles F. Johnson, aide-de-camp, and T. J. Clay, acting aide; Majs. Alexander Casseday, acting inspector-general and S. K. Hays, quartermaster; Capt. R. C. Wintersmith, commissary of subsistence; Major Davidson, chief of artillery; Messrs. J. N. Galleher [afterward Bishop of Louisiana], acting aide; Moore, acting topographical officer; J. Walker Taylor, commanding a detachment of guides, and D. P. Buckner, volunteer aide." Major Casseday died at Camp Chase not long afterward from the effects of exposure at Fort Donelson.

The Eighth Kentucky regiment did not come under General Buckner's observation, but both General Bushrod Johnson, division commander, and Colonel Simonton, brigade commander, refer to its gallant action, while Colonel Lyon says that "no officers or men could have acted more gallantly than did those of the Eighth Kentucky at all times during the three days' fight." Out of 312 men, his loss was 17 killed and 46 wounded, while the Second Kentucky lost 80 killed and wounded out of five or six hundred.

CHAPTER VI

SHILOH CAMPAIGN — EFFECT OF THE SURRENDER OF FORT DONELSON — EVACUATION OF BOWLING GREEN AND NASHVILLE — UNJUST OUTBURST OF INDIGNATION AGAINST GENERAL JOHNSTON — GENERAL BUELL OCCUPIES NASHVILLE — REORGANIZATION OF CONFEDERATE ARMY AT MURFREESBORO — ASSIGNMENT OF KENTUCKY TROOPS — GENERAL JOHNSTON'S SUCCESSFUL MOVEMENT TO CORINTH, MISS. — JUNCTION WITH BEAUREGARD, BRAGG AND POLK — RAPID PREPARATIONS FOR ADVANCE — GENERAL GRANT AT PITTSBURG LANDING — GENERAL BUELL MOVING TO JOIN HIM — GENERAL JOHNSTON ADVANCES TO GIVE BATTLE TO GENERAL GRANT — BATTLE OF SHILOH — PART TAKEN BY KENTUCKY CONFEDERATE TROOPS — THEIR GALLANTRY AND SEVERE LOSSES — DEATH OF GENERAL JOHNSTON — HIS LAST LETTER TO PRESIDENT DAVIS — DEATH OF GOVERNOR GEORGE W. JOHNSON — RETREAT TO CORINTH

THE effect of the fall of Fort Donelson was stunning to the South, especially as it came close upon the heels of the report of a great victory. On the night of the battle General Johnston received dispatches announcing that the Confederates had won the battle. At daylight on the 16th came the announcement of the surrender. In Nashville the excitement and tumult were intense, and all over the South there was a mingled feeling of disappointment and indignation. The brunt of the blame fell upon General Johnston, who, knowing that time would vindicate him, bore it calmly and made the best dispositions to meet the calamity. He was calm under the animadversions cast upon him in the Confederate Congress and by the turbulent populace in Nashville. He moved his forces to the south of Nashville, organized the refugees and stragglers from Fort Donelson and began the evacuation of the capital of Tennessee by removing the army supplies. The proper precautions were taken to prevent a sudden attack on the city by the gunboats, and in a few days the morale of his army, reduced fully one-half by the disaster at Donelson, was restored. He had long been aware of the danger, and before evacuating Bowling Green had foreseen the possible necessity of falling behind the Cumberland, and in extremity, the Tennessee. His plan was fully matured, and he had selected Corinth, Miss., just south of the great bend of the Tennessee, as the point at which he would rally, and from which with the concentration of all available forces he would move to give battle to the Federal forces. By the 22d, the evacuation of Nashville was complete, and on the 23d the advance guard of the Federal army from Bowling Green appeared at Edgefield on the north side of the Cumberland. A deputation of the citizens, with the mayor, went out to negotiate, and on the 25th the formal surrender of the city to General Buell took place.

On the 23d of February, the organization of General Johnston's forces being completed at Murfreesboro, he issued an order announcing the reorganization of the army and assuming command. It consisted of Hardee's division, composed of Hindman's and Cleburne's brigades; Crittenden's division, of Carroll's and Statham's brigades; Pillow's division, of Wood's and Bowen's brigades; and the Reserve under Gen. John C. Breckinridge. This latter comprised the following commands: Third Kentucky, Col. A. P. Thompson; Fourth Kentucky, Col. R. P. Trabue; Fifth Kentucky (afterward called the Ninth), Col. Thomas H. Hunt; Sixth Kentucky, Col. Joseph H. Lewis; Col. Crew's regiment, Clifton's battalion, Hale's battalion, Helm's cavalry battalion, Morgan's squadron of cavalry, Nelson's cavalry, Lyon's (Cobb's) battery. Col. N. B. Forrest's cavalry, and Col. John A. Wharton's cavalry (Eighth Texas), were unattached. On the 28th of February, no movement from Nashville having been meanwhile made against General Johnston, he put his army in motion for Decatur, Ala., via Shelbyville, reaching the former place on the 10th of March. Here the Tennessee river, then at flood-height, was crossed, and by the 25th of March General Johnston completed the concentration of his army at Corinth. This included, in addition to the troops brought by him, the command of General Polk, which had evacuated Columbus on the 2d of March, and General Bragg's corps of 10,000 from Pensacola, which together with other smaller detachments made about 40,000 men.

A corresponding movement had meanwhile taken place on the part of the Federal forces. General Grant had on the 10th of March begun his expedition up the Tennessee river, and on the 17th the greater part of his army, now augmented to nearly 50,000 effectives, was in camp at and near Pittsburg Landing on the southwest side of the Tennessee, twenty-three miles northeast of Corinth. On the 15th of March General Buell, with his army of 37,000, marched from Nashville for the same point by way of Columbia and Waynesboro, while Gen. O. M. Mitchel with a corps of 18,000 marched south to Huntsville and Decatur to seize the Memphis & Charleston railroad. Such was the situation, with General Grant resting in fancied security and awaiting the arrival of General Buell to move southward, with no thought of danger, when General Johnston, hoping to strike him before Buell should effect a junction, moved out from Corinth on the 3rd of April. He had said in response to the clamor following the evacuation of Kentucky and Tennessee that if he could effect a concentration of his scattered forces, those who declaimed against him would be without an argument. He was now about to redeem his word. How fully at Shiloh he did it, and in an instant won enduring fame, history has recorded with indelible pen.*

Owing to continued rains and difficulty of moving his army, the battle was delayed at least a day, but taking his adversary completely by surprise on the morning of Sunday, April 6th, he lived long enough to see his army in the full tide of victory. A few hours more of life would have secured the surrender of the opposing army. What would ultimately have happened had he survived is left to the judgment of those who can best comprehend the genius of a general who had so thoroughly vindicated his capacity for aggressive as well as defensive operations. How all the fruits of victory were lost by his death have, together with the details of the great battle, been faithfully told by his son in a memoir as valuable for its historical accuracy as for its faithful portraiture of a noble life and character.**

The Confederate troops which fought at Shiloh were organized as follows: First corps, General Polk; Second corps, General Bragg; Third corps, General Hardee; Reserve, General Breckinridge. The last is the only one in regard to which any detail will be given here. It was composed of the following: First brigade, Col. R. P. Trabue; Second brigade, Brig.-Gen. J. S. Bowen;

* For General Johnston's last letter to President Davis, battle order, etc., see Appendix B.

** The life of Gen. Albert Sidney Johnston, embracing his services in the armies of the United States, the Republic of Texas and the Confederate States by William Preston Johnston. New York, D. Appleton & Co., 1878.

Third brigade, Brig.-Gen. W. S. Statham; Morgan's squadron of cavalry. The First brigade consisted of the Fourth Alabama battalion, Thirty-first Alabama regiment; Lieutenant-Colonel Crews' Tennessee battalion; Third Kentucky regiment, Lieut.-Col. Ben Anderson commanding; Fourth Kentucky regiment, Lieut.-Col. A. R. Hynes commanding; Ninth Kentucky regiment, Col. T. H. Hunt; Sixth Kentucky regiment, Col. J. H. Lewis; Byrne's battery; Cobb's battery; in all about 2,400 men. The battle of Shiloh was begun at daylight by Hardee's corps, and it was not long until nearly the whole Confederate force was engaged, the general position from left to right being Hardee, Polk, Bragg and Breckinridge. As is not uncommon in military experience, the reserve was early in action. Colonel Trabue, with the Kentucky brigade, was sent as reinforcement to General Hardee's right, on the left of General Polk's corps, while the remainder of General Breckinridge's division moved to the support of the extreme right. It was thus that the Kentucky troops found themselves in one of the most stubbornly contested parts of the field, being pitted against the command of General Sherman, where was found the most stubborn resistance. In the first assault Lieutenant-Colonel Anderson and Major Johnston, of the Third Kentucky, were wounded, and Captains Stone, Pearce and Emerson, Lieutenant Bagwell, commanding company, and Acting Lieutenant White, of that regiment, were killed; while Captain Bowman, Adjutant McGoodwin and Lieutenants Ross and Ridgeway were wounded. Later the brigade had a prolonged contest with a heavy force of Ohio and Iowa troops, and drove them with a charge, the Kentucky troops singing their battle song, "Cheer, boys, cheer; we'll march away to battle," and driving everything before them. The loss was heavy, Captains Ben Desha and John W. Caldwell being severely, and Adjt. Wm. Bell, of the Ninth Kentucky, mortally wounded. In the same regiment Capt. James R. Bright, Lieut. J. L. Moore and R. M. Lemmons were wounded. In the Fourth Kentucky, Capt. John A. Adair, Lieut. John Bird Rogers, commanding company, and Lieut. Robert Dunn, were severely wounded, while Capt. W. Lee Earned, of the Sixth Kentucky, was mortally wounded. This success led soon after to the capture of General Prentiss' Federal command, and by a happy conjunction, just as Colonel Trabue entered the camp from the left, General Breckinridge came in from the right. The prisoners, numbering about 3,000, were sent to the rear in charge of Crews' battalion of Colonel Trabue's brigade. By this stroke of good fortune the Sixth and Ninth Kentucky were enabled to change their old muskets for Enfield rifles.

The foregoing has been collated from the report of Colonel Trabue, Rebellion Records, Vol. X, page 614. It is to be regretted that no extended report by General Breckinridge was ever made, or if made has never been found. The following is the only one relating to the battle:

Hdqrs. Reserve Corps, Army of the Mississippi,
April 17, 1862.

Colonel: I have the honor to make the following statement of the small-arms, cannon, etc., captured from the enemy in the battles of the 6th and 7th by the Reserve corps, exclusive of the cavalry, from whom there is no report; small-arms 1,393, swords 11, cannon 4 pieces. The small-arms are now in the hands of my men, most of them taken from dead and wounded enemies, and substituted for rifles or guns before in our possession. The four pieces were hauled several miles off the field and within our lines by Captain Rutledge, commanding battery in Statham's brigade, and it is confidently believed form a part of the captured cannon now at Corinth.

My command did not stop in their camps, but moved on under orders, and I think did its full share upon the line of its operations in the work, of which captured cannon, flags, small-arms and prisoners were the result.

Respectfully,
JOHN C. BRECKINRIDGE,
Brigadier-General Commanding.

In a sketch of the Kentucky brigade, written by Gen. Geo. B. Hodge, General Breckinridge's adjutant-general at Shiloh, occurs the following graphic description: "Two o'clock had arrived and the whole army was now or had been for hours engaged, with the exception of Bowen's and Statham's brigades of the Reserve corps. The enemy had been driven through and from half of his camps, but refused to give back further. Having given way on his right and left wings he had massed his force heavily in the center, and poured an almost unremitting hail of fire, murderous beyond description, from his covert of trees and bushes, when General Breckinridge was ordered up to break his line. Having been most of the day in observation on the Hamburg road, marching in column of regiments, the reserve was now moved by the right flank, until opposite the point of attack, then deployed rapidly into line of battle, Statham's brigade forming the right and Bowen's the left. The long slope of the ridge was here abruptly broken by a succession of small hills or undulations of about fifty feet in height, dividing the rolling country from the river bottom; and behind the crest of these last the enemy was concealed. Opposite them, at the distance of seventy-five yards, was another long swell or hillock, the summit of which it was necessary to attain in order to open fire, and to this elevation the reserve moved in order of battle at double-quick. In an instant the opposing height was one sheet of flame. Battle's Tennessee regiment on the extreme right gallantly maintained itself, pushing forward under a withering fire and establishing itself well in advance. Little's Tennessee regiment next to it delivered its fire at random and inefficiently, became disordered and retired in confusion down the slope. Three times it was rallied by its lieutenant-colonel, assisted by Col. T. T. Hawkins, aide-de-camp to General Breckinridge, and by the adjutant-general, and carried up the slope only to be as often repulsed and driven back; the regiment of the enemy opposed to it in the intervals directing an oblique fire upon Battle's regiment, now contending against overwhelming odds. The crisis of the contest had come; there were no more reserves, and General Breckinridge determined to charge. Calling the staff around him, he communicated to them his intentions and remarked that he with them would lead it. They were all Kentuckians, and though it was not their privilege to fight that day with the Kentucky brigade, they were yet men who knew how to die bravely among strangers, and some at least would live to do justice to the rest. The commander-in-chief, General Johnston, rode up at this juncture and learning the contemplated movement, determined to accompany it. Placing himself on the left of Little's regiment, his commanding figure in full uniform conspicuous to every eye, he awaited the signal. General Breckinridge, disposing his staff along the line, rode to the right of the same regiment. Then with a wild shout, which rose above the din of battle, on swept the line through a storm of fire, over the hill, across the intervening ravine and up the slope occupied by the enemy. Nothing could withstand it. The enemy broke and fled for a half mile, hotly pursued until he reached the shelter of his batteries. Well did the Kentuckians sustain that day their honor and their fame! Of the little band of officers who started on that forlorn hope but one was unscathed, the gallant Breckinridge himself. Colonel Hawkins was wounded in the face; Captain Allen's leg was torn to pieces by a shell; the horses of the fearless boy, J. Cabell Breckinridge, and of the adjutant-general were killed under them, and General Johnston was lifted dying from his saddle. It may be doubted whether the success, brilliant as it was, decisive as it was, compensated for the loss of the great captain."

While the dramatic effect of this description is heightened by the statement that General Johnston received his death-wound in this charge, his biographer says that he was but slightly wounded, and that the bullet which cut the thread of his life was a stray one which struck him after the charge and while he was in the rear of Breckinridge's line in a position of comparative security.

When darkness closed the battle of the first day, there was but little territory and comparatively few Federal troops between the advanced Confederate lines and the river, and it is not without reason to believe that the remnant would have been forced to surrender but for the timely arrival of Gen. Wm. Nelson, of General Buell's army who, with characteristic vigor crossed the river and with Colonel Ammen's brigade of fresh troops, pushed to the front and checked the Confederate advance. His official report confirms the demoralized condition of General Grant's army. He says, "I found cowering under the river bank when I crossed, from 7,000 to 10,000 men frantic with fright and utterly demoralized, who received my gallant division with cries that 'we are whipped,' 'cut to pieces,' etc. They were insensible to shame and sarcasm, for I tried both on them; and indignant at such poltroonery I asked permission to fire on the knaves." All who know the demoralizing effect of defeat upon the bravest of men will condemn the severity of this language, indicating an unrestrained violence of temper, which less than six months later cost Nelson his life.

While the Confederates were elated with victory and expecting to complete it, they were ordered to halt by General Beauregard, who had succeeded to the command. Next morning the Federals, finding their front clear, advanced with the fresh troops of General Buell's army, and the operations of the day consisted chiefly in a stubborn retreat by the Confederates, who fell back slowly, fighting with persistence and vigor. Among the commands most heavily engaged was the Kentucky brigade, which for four or five hours held its position near Shiloh Church against a large force of the enemy. Its losses were heavy. Among the killed were Maj. Thomas B. Monroe, Jr., Adjutant Forman and Lieutenant Dooley of the Fourth Kentucky. Lieutenant-Colonel Hynes, Capts. Jos. P. Nuckols, Ben J. Monroe, T. W. Thompson and J. M. Fitzhenry, and Lieuts. John B. Moore, Thomas Steele, S. O. Peyton and George B. Burnley were among the wounded. Detailing these casualties the report of Colonel Trabue adds: "And here also fell that noble patriot, Gov. George W. Johnson, after having fought in the ranks of Capt. Ben Monroe's company (E, Fourth Kentucky) with unfaltering bravery from early Sunday morning to this unhappy moment." Governor Johnson had accompanied the army on its retreat from Bowling Green, and went to the battlefield on the staff of General Breckinridge on Sunday morning; but when the Kentucky brigade was detached, he accompanied it and served on the staff of Colonel Trabue. At half past nine o'clock his horse was killed and he then, with characteristic spirit, took a musket and served as a member of Capt. Ben J. Monroe's company. Being mortally wounded on the afternoon of Monday by a minie-ball which passed through his body just below the median line, such was his vitality that he lay on the battlefield until the following day, when General McCook, in riding over the field, found him and had him carried to a boat at the landing. They had met at the Charleston convention. He survived the night, being kindly cared for, and was able to send messages to his family, leaving in his last words a testimony that his only aim had been his country's good. He was in his fiftieth year and had filled many positions of honor, but had declined the nomination for lieutenant-governor and for Congress when it was equivalent to an election. He was a man of peace, but of the metal to follow his convictions wherever duty led. General Beauregard, in his report of the battle, thus refers to his death: "I deeply regret to record also the death of Hon. George W. Johnson, provisional governor of Kentucky, who went into action with the Kentucky troops and continually inspired them by his words and example. Having his horse shot under him on Sunday, he entered the ranks of a Kentucky regiment on Monday and fell mortally wounded toward the close of the day. Not his State alone, but the whole Confederacy, has sustained a great loss in the death of this brave, upright and able man." "In the conflicts of this day," continues Colonel Trabue, "Lieut.-Col. Robert A.

Johnston, after exemplary conduct, was wounded, Capt. William Mitchell was killed, and Capt. George A. King and Lieutenants Gillum, Harding and Schaub were wounded; all of the Fifth Kentucky. In the Sixth Kentucky, Lieutenant-Colonel Cofer, a cool, brave and efficient officer, was wounded; Capt. W. W. Bagby and Lieut. M. E. Aull were mortally wounded; Capts. D. E. McKendree and John G. Hudson were likewise wounded, as were also Lieuts. L. M. Tucker and Charles Dawson, the last named of whom was taken prisoner. Late in the evening of this second day, General Breckinridge, with the Kentucky brigade and Statham's, and some cavalry, undertook to check the enemy and cover the retreat. This was a hard duty, exposed as the command had been and wasted as they were by the loss of more than half their numbers; but the general was equal to the great undertaking, and his officers and men shared his devotion to duty." The loss of the brigade was 844 out of a total of something less than 2,400; the Third Kentucky losing 174, Fourth 213, Fifth 134, Sixth 108, Cobb's battery 37, Byrne's 14. Colonel Trabue notes particularly the gallant service of Cobb's and Byrne's batteries, both of which made names for themselves second to none in that arm of the service. The horses of Cobb's battery were nearly all killed on the first day, but he saved his guns, while on the second day Byrne's battery had been so depleted by the casualties of battle that at one time he was assisted in the service of his guns by volunteers from the infantry of the brigade. The Seventh Kentucky infantry, Col. Charles Wickliffe, served during the battle in Col. W. H. Stephens' brigade of Cheatham's division. Colonel Wickliffe was mortally wounded and succeeded by Lieut.-Col. W. D. Lannom. Later Col. Edward Crossland became commander of the Seventh and continued so during the war.

CHAPTER VII

REORGANIZATION OF THE ARMY AT CORINTH — KENTUCKY COMMANDS — GENERAL BRECKINRIDGE SENT TO VICKSBURG — IN THE TRENCHES THERE — BATTLE OF BATON ROUGE — LOSS OF RAM ARKANSAS — FAILURE OF EXPEDITION IN CONSEQUENCE — GENERAL BRECKINRIDGE DEFEATS FEDERAL FORCE — LOSS IN KILLED AND WOUNDED — CAMP AT COMITE RIVER—DEPLETION OF COMMAND BY SICKNESS — GENERAL BRECKINRIDGE INVITED BY GENERAL BRAGG TO COMMAND A DIVISION IN PENDING KENTUCKY CAMPAIGN — DECLINES TO LEAVE HIS TROOPS IN THEIR EXTREMITY — EFFORTS TO HAVE HIM SENT WITH THEM — ORDER FINALLY ISSUED — OBSTRUCTIONS INTERPOSED — FATAL DELAY — HE MARCHES FROM KNOXVILLE FOR KENTUCKY — BRAGG'S RETREAT FROM KENTUCKY COMPELS HIS RETURN

THE retreat of the Confederate army in the direction of Corinth was successfully covered by General Breckinridge's command, the pursuit not having been prosecuted more than five or six miles. The falling back was leisurely, and it was not until the 11th of April that the Kentucky brigade reached Corinth. In the reorganization of the army which took place here, General Breckinridge's Reserve corps was composed of four brigades, two of which, the first and second, comprised the Kentucky troops. The First brigade, commanded by Brig.-Gen. J. M. Hawes, consisted of the Forty-first Alabama, Fourth Kentucky, Ninth Kentucky, Hale's Alabama regiment, Clifton's Alabama battalion and Byrne's battery, but the latter soon disbanding, Hudson's battery took its place. The Second brigade, commanded by Brig.-Gen. William Preston, consisted of the Third, Sixth and Seventh Kentucky regiments, and Cobb's battery. The Third brigade, comprising two Arkansas, one Mississippi and one Missouri regiment, was given to Brig.-Gen. Ben Hardin Helm. But soon after, General Hawes being assigned to the Trans-Mississippi department, General Helm was placed in command of the First brigade. About the first of June the Confederate army fell back to Tupelo, Miss., and from there the Kentucky troops were transferred to General Van Dorn's department, and on the 30th took their place in the trenches at Vicksburg. The operations against his point at that time were by the fleet, without any land force, and were confined to the bombardment of the place by heavy guns. The most destructive enemy to the Kentucky troops was the climate, from which they suffered greatly.

On the 27th of July, General Breckinridge was sent to make an attack on Baton Rouge, where was a Federal force of three or four thousand, the purpose being to have the Confederate ram Arkansas co-operate in the expedition. His report, to be found in the Rebellion Records, Vol. XV, page 76, states that he left with less than 4,000 men, who in two days were reduced by sickness to 3,400. He went by rail to Tangipahoa, whence Baton Rouge is 55 miles west. On the 4th he arrived at the Comite river, within 10 miles of Baton Rouge, and at 11 p. m. on the same night he marched for that point, reaching its vicinity before daylight on the 5th. While waiting for daylight a serious accident occurred. A party of rangers, placed in rear of the artillery, "leaked through" and riding forward encountered the enemy's pickets, causing exchange of shots. Galloping back they produced confusion, which led to rapid firing, during which General Helm was dangerously wounded by the fall of his horse, and his aide, Lieut. A. H. Todd, was killed. Helm was a brother-in-law of Mrs. Lincoln; Lieutenant Todd was her half-brother. Captain Roberts, of the Second Kentucky, was dangerously wounded, and two of Captain Cobb's three guns rendered for the time useless. The enemy thus aroused, awaited attack in two lines. Our troops advanced in single line with strong reserves at intervals. The Second division, General Ruggles, advanced to the attack on the left with impetuosity, cheering and driving the enemy before it. General Preston having been left sick at Vicksburg, Col. A. P. Thompson led the First brigade of the division, and was seriously wounded in the charge. The First division, General Clark, composed of one brigade under Col. Thomas H. Hunt and one under Col. T. B. Smith, Twentieth Tennessee, drove the enemy on the right until after several hours' fighting he had fallen back to a grove just back of the penitentiary. The fight was hot and stubborn, and here the division met the greatest loss. Colonel Hunt was shot down, and at the suggestion of General Clark, Capt. John A. Buckner, General Breckinridge's adjutant-general, was placed in command of the brigade. Shortly afterward General Clark received a wound thought to be mortal, when under some misapprehension the First brigade of his division began to fall back, but rallied, and in a renewed attack the enemy was driven back and disappeared in the town. Maj. J. C. Wickliffe commanded the Ninth regiment, Col. J. W. Caldwell having been injured in the accident of the early morning and obliged to retire. Here the Confederates suffered from the fire of the fleet, but in the end the enemy were completely routed and did not again appear during the day. It was now 10 o'clock, and they had listened in vain for the guns of the ram Arkansas, which, it proved, had disabled her machinery when four miles above Baton Rouge, and, to prevent her falling into the hands of the Federal fleet near by, had been abandoned and set on fire by her officers. General Breckinridge, in view of this failure of co-operation, suspended further attack, and being wholly unmolested, withdrew to his camp at Comite river. His total loss was 467 killed, wounded and missing. From the heat of the weather and scarcity of drinking water the men suffered greatly. General Breckinridge said: "The enemy were well clothed and their encampments showed the presence of every comfort and even luxury. Our men had little transportation, indifferent food and no shelter. Half of them had no coats, and hundreds of them were without either shoes or socks. Yet no troops ever behaved with greater gallantry and even reckless audacity. What can make this difference, unless it be the sublime courage inspired by a just cause?"

Within a few days General Breckinridge sent a small force and occupied Port Hudson above Baton Rouge, which became afterward a fortified place second only to Vicksburg. The effect of the climate on his troops was fearful, not in the number of deaths, but in disabling them for duty. A report of Surg. J. W. Thompson, of the First brigade, in which were the Third, Sixth and Seventh Kentucky, shows that on arriving at Vicksburg, June 30th, there were 1,822 men on duty; on leaving Vicksburg July 27th, 1,252; on duty after the battle of Baton Rouge, 584.

It was just one week after the battle that the writer of this history visited the camp. He found General Breckinridge encamped on the Comite river, a small stream with low banks and flat, wooded lands adjacent, with every malarial indication. The wan, enfeebled aspect of his men was pitiable to look upon, and he was chafing under the orders which held them inactive in such a pestilential locality. The writer had come from General Bragg, then at Chattanooga preparing to move into Kentucky, and brought with him the following letter:

Chattanooga, August 8, 1862.

Maj.-Gen. J. C. Breckinridge:

My dear General: Having but time for a note for Mr. Johnston I must leave him to explain what he knows or suspects of the future. My army has promised to make me military governor of Ohio in 90 days (Seward's time for crushing the rebellion), and as they cannot do that without passing your home, I have thought you would like to have an escort to visit your family.

Seriously, I should be much better satisfied were you with me on the impending campaign. Your influence in Kentucky would be equal to an extra division to my army; but you can readily see my embarrassment. Your division cannot be brought here now. To separate you from it might be injurious and even unpleasant to you, and not satisfactory to General Van Dorn. If you desire it, and General Van Dorn will consent, you shall come at once. A command is ready for you, and I shall hope to see your eyes beam again at the command "Forward" as they did at Shiloh, in the midst of our greatest success. General Lovell is disengaged and might replace you, or I would cheerfully give General Van Dorn any one I could spare. It would also please me to see General Preston along, but I fear to make too great a draft on your command.

If agreeable to yourself and General Van Dorn you have no time to lose. We only await our train and the capture of the forces at Cumberland Gap, both of which we hope to hear from very soon.

Our prospects were never more encouraging.

Most respectfully and truly yours,

BRAXTON BRAGG.

General Breckinridge was eager to go into Kentucky, but said that even if Van Dorn would give his consent he would not voluntarily leave his men in the condition they were, and so advised General Bragg, urging that he be permitted to take with him his Kentucky command. The writer bore his answer, urged it upon General Van Dorn in person at his headquarters at Jackson, Miss., and upon the President at Richmond by letter. A few days later the Kentucky senators and representatives in the Confederate Congress addressed President Davis as follows:

Richmond, Va., August 18, 1862.

Hon. Jefferson Davis,

President of the Confederate States:

Sir: Having such information as satisfies us that the Western army is now moving in two columns in the direction of Kentucky, one column under the command of General Bragg from Chattanooga, and the other under the immediate command of Maj.-Gen. E. Kirby Smith, and entertaining no doubt that General Smith will be able in a short time to reach the very heart of the more wealthy and populous portion of our State, and believing from information derived from sources entitled to credit that a large majority of the people of the State sympathize with the South and that a large proportion of the young men will at once join our army, we regard it as of the very highest importance that as many of the officers in the service of the government as are from the State of Kentucky and who have heretofore held position in and had the confidence of the people of the State, should be in Kentucky when the army reaches there. We do not regard this as so important looking merely to military results, but we desire to present it to your consideration in its political aspects. We have now in Kentucky a civil government opposed to us; elections have recently been held in which the voice of the people was suppressed by the order of the military governor of the State; soldiers were placed around the ballot-boxes; the people were not permitted to vote without taking odious oaths prescribed by the military authorities unknown to and in derogation of the Constitution; candidates who were the favorites of the majority of the people, who would have been elected, were peremptorily ordered to at once withdraw from the canvass under penalty of being immediately sent to a military prison, and the officers of the election were directed not to place the names of candidates on the poll-books unless they were known to be loyal to the Federal government, of which loyalty there was no standard except the caprice, the passion or the interest of the officers themselves.

You will at once perceive that should we get military possession of the State one of the first things to be done will be to overthrow this usurpation, and to give to the people of the State an opportunity of establishing such a government as they may desire and of electing such officers to execute the powers of government as they may prefer. It then becomes important that the citizens of Kentucky who have the confidence of the great body of the people, and who have been intimately associated with them both in private life and in the conduct of public affairs, should return to the State to aid and co-operate with the people in their efforts to overthrow the despotism that now oppresses them and re-establish constitutional free government in the State. We are fully convinced that their presence among their old friends and fellow citizens at this time would be attended with the happiest results both to the people of the State and to the Confederacy; and we would therefore most respectfully suggest and recommend that as many of the officers and soldiers from Kentucky in the service as can be spared for the purpose with a due regard to other exigencies and interests, should be temporarily withdrawn from other duty and attached to the army entering that State.

We would therefore respectfully suggest that Major-General Breckinridge, with his division generals, Buckner and Marshall, be sent to Kentucky.

We have the honor to be very respectfully, Your obedient servants,

JOHN W. CROCKETT,
GEO. W. EWING,
H. C. BURNETT,
R. J. BRECKINRIDGE,
E. M. BRUCE,
HENRY E. READ,
W. E. SIMMS,
W. B. MACHEN,
GEO. B. HODGE,
JAMES S. CHRISMAN.

President Davis, on receipt of this letter, renewed his order already given directing that General Breckinridge should accompany the movement. A few days later General Hardee sent him the following dispatch:

Chattanooga, Tenn., August 23, 1862.

Major-General Breckinridge:

Come here if possible. I have a splendid division for you to lead into Kentucky, to which will be attached all the men General Van Dorn can spare to bring with you.

W. J. HARDEE, Major-General.

To which General Breckinridge replied :

Jackson, Miss., August 25, 1862.

Major-General Hardee, Chattanooga:

Reserve the division for me. I will leave here in a few days with a small force of Kentuckians and Tennesseeans.

JOHN C. BRECKINRIDGE.

General Bragg left Chattanooga for Kentucky on the 28th of August. The day before he started, he wrote as follows:

Chattanooga, August 27, 1862. Major-General Breckinridge:

My Dear General: We leave for your beloved home tomorrow. Would that you were with us. Your division is ready for you as soon as you join, but you must hurry up to overtake us. Buell is anxious apparently to get to Cincinnati before us, but we envy him the honor. General Jones (Samuel) had orders to organize, arm and equip all stragglers, recovered sick, and those absent from leave and have them ready to join you. The quartermaster department has orders to be ready to send you on. Move with 100 rounds of ammunition and twenty-five days' rations. We go by way of Sparta and Burkesville into the heart of Kentucky.

Yours most truly,

BRAXTON BRAGG.

The above and much more correspondence on the subject will be found in the Rebellion Records, Vol. XVI, Part II. All of it indicates Bragg's earnest desire to have General Breckinridge with him, and the equally ardent wish of the latter to respond. But it was not to be. General Van Dorn had in view a campaign against General Rosecrans which later culminated in disaster at Iuka and Corinth, and did not wish to give up General Breckinridge. He was detained in Mississippi until President Davis, being apprised of the situation, gave peremptory orders which secured his release. Even then he was hampered with the duty of collecting at Knoxville all the recently exchanged prisoners, furloughed men and convalescents, so that he did not get to Knoxville until October 3d, as shown by a dispatch of that date saying, "I have just arrived here with 2,500 men, all that General Van Dorn would let me have. About 2,000 exchanged prisoners will arrive in a day or two." Had he been permitted at the start to take with him his old skeleton regiments and push forward, effecting a junction with Bragg in central Kentucky, he would have recruited them to a maximum, and might have given or left for us a different history of that period. As it was, vexatious delays still further detained him, and it was not until October 14th that he was able to leave Knoxville. When he had reached within twenty-eight miles of Cumberland Gap on the 17th, he received an order from General Bragg written at Barboursville, Ky., October 14th, directing him to return to Knoxville. His further operation's will appear in a later chapter.

CHAPTER VIII

OPENING OF THE SUMMER CAMPAIGN IN 1862 — RELATIVE STRENGTH AND POSITION OF FEDERAL AND CONFEDERATE FORCES — GENERAL BUELL'S MOVEMENT FROM CORINTH FOR THE REDUCTION OF EAST TENNESSEE — GENERAL G. W. MORGAN'S ADVANCE ON CUMBERLAND GAP — ITS FINAL OCCUPATION BY HIM — GENERAL BRAGG SUCCEEDS GENERAL BEAUREGARD AT TUPELO — GENERAL E. KIRBY SMITH IN EAST TENNESSEE — HIS CRITICAL POSITION — GENERAL BUELL THREATENS CHATTANOOGA — HIS SUCCESS SEEMS ASSURED — GENERAL POPE SLURS THE CONFEDERATE ARMY AT TUPELO — GENERAL BRAGG CONTEMPLATES MOVING NORTHWARD TO STRIKE BUELL IN FLANK — PLAN ABANDONED AS IMPRACTICABLE — ANOTHER BRILLIANT STRATEGIC MOVE DECIDED ON

THE current of the narrative has been somewhat broken and the sequence of events anticipated, in order to group the foregoing facts in what seems the best form for a good understanding of a subject which has never been made clear to Kentuckians, and in reference to which there has been no little incorrect representation. Pending the events which have been detailed as participated in by the Kentucky troops under General Breckinridge, important movements were in progress in other parts of the department of the Mississippi which were soon to change the whole aspect of affairs. The two opposing armies, which confronted each other at Corinth after Shiloh, passed through a season of inaction in which no definite policy could be discerned, and no considerable achievement was performed by either. Each seemed to wait on the other. Memphis had fallen, and the Federal forces were in undisputed possession of all Tennessee west of the Cumberland mountains.

They also occupied north Alabama and north Mississippi, Missouri, and the State of Arkansas north of the Arkansas river. The Mississippi river was open from the north to Vicksburg and from the gulf to Port Hudson.

This was the Federal situation on the 10th of June, 1862. General Halleck, in command of the department of the West, had at and near Corinth, Miss., an army of more than 100,000 men under Generals Grant, Buell and Pope. The Confederate army under General Beauregard was at Tupelo, Miss., forty-five miles south of Corinth, and numbered 45,000 men of all arms. The Confederates were content, apparently, to remain on the defensive, while the commander of the Federal forces hesitated to penetrate further south with a climate dangerous to his troops, a line of supply difficult to maintain, and with unprotected flanks inviting assaults from an enterprising cavalry. But as nothing is so demoralizing as inactivity in an army, and popular clamor at the North was loud in its demands for a more active campaign, the Federal commander suddenly roused himself from the lethargy which seemed to have been superinduced by the languor of the summer's heat. The activity of General McClellan in the east had been at this time in marked contrast, and confidence had grown sanguine that he would succeed in his operations against Richmond. But McClellan's advance had resulted in his defeat at Seven Pines on May 30th. Lee's great victories in the Seven Days' battles followed, and the Federal armies were forced to retreat. Political necessity and the popular discontent required that the army of the West should shake off its lethargy.

A campaign in the West on a large scale was soon projected. On the 9th of June General Halleck had notified the war department at Washington that he would send all forces not required to hold the Memphis & Charleston railroad to reinforce General Curtis at Helena, Ark., and to East Tennessee, to which Secretary Stanton replied on the 11th: "The President is greatly gratified at your contemplated movements mentioned in your telegram two days ago." At last it seemed that the Utopian scheme of rescuing East Tennessee from the Confederates was to be made the chief feature of the campaign. On the 10th General Halleck revoked his previous orders which had divided the army into right, center and left wings and directed Generals Grant, Buell and Pope to resume command of their respective corps, viz.: the armies of the Tennessee, of the Ohio and of the Mississippi.

General Buell's army of the Ohio consisted at that time of the Second division, Gen. A. McD. McCook, comprising the brigades of Generals Rosecrans, Richard W. Johnson and Colonel Frederick Stambaugh, with three batteries of artillery: the Third division, Maj.-Gen. O. M. Mitchel, composed of the brigades of Generals Turchin, Sill and Lytle, the Fourth Ohio cavalry and three batteries of artillery: the Fourth division, Brig.-Gen. William Nelson, containing brigades of Generals Ammen, Grose and

Manson and three batteries of artillery: the Fifth division, Brig.-Gen. Thomas L. Crittenden, containing brigades of Gens. J. T. Boyle and VanCleve and two batteries of artillery: the Sixth division, Brig.-Gen. T. J. Wood, containing brigades of Generals Hascall, Garfield and Wagner and three batteries of artillery: the Seventh division, Brig.-Gen. Geo. W. Morgan, containing Carter's, Spears', De Courcy's and Baird's brigades, the Sixth cavalry and three batteries. Besides these organizations there were three independent infantry brigades commanded by General Negley, Colonel Lester and General Dumont, with four reserve batteries, a brigade of cavalry, eleven unattached regiments and three batteries of artillery. This by the tri-monthly report of June 10th showed present for duty 2,877 officers and 57,822 men.

On the 12th of June General Buell's department was announced in orders as embracing the States of Kentucky and Tennessee east of the Tennessee river, except Forts Henry and Donelson, and such portions of north Alabama and Georgia as were or might be occupied by the Federal troops. About the same time General Buell was directed to move eastward and take possession of East Tennessee General Halleck preferred that he should go by way of Chattanooga, but left it entirely to General Buell's judgment to select his route, and as will be seen later, he gave preference to the more northern route by way of McMinnville, about half way between Nashville and Chattanooga. As part of this plan Gen. George W. Morgan had already been sent with his division to Cumberland Gap, to co-operate by a movement upon Knoxville from that point. As the operations of the armies of Generals Grant and Pope will not come under further observation in these pages, it is not necessary to enter into details as to their organization. The former was assigned to Memphis and to the relief of General Curtis in Arkansas, and the latter to Corinth, apparently to watch, if not to move against, the Confederate army at Tupelo.

Against such an organization,with such reserves to draw upon, such resources of equipment and supply, and such facilities for transportation, the student of to-day with the full official publications before him will wonder that any further effective resistance could be opposed to the occupation of any part of the South in possession of the Confederates, upon which a movement should be made. Since the disastrous loss of Kentucky and Tennessee, and the battles of Fort Donelson and Shiloh, in which, apart from the territorial loss, the sacrifice of life both in number and merit had been grievous, there had been no Confederate victory to offset these multiplied disasters; and by all the rules which would seem to govern human action it would be inferred that the hopelessness of despair would have settled down upon the Southern people and rendered them incapable of farther resistance. But it was not so Instead of being overwhelmed in spirit, their courage and fertility of resource rose, and new and more energetic means of resistance were projected which turned defeat into victory, and wrung even from their bitterest detractors reluctant applause.

The body of the Confederate strength, as has been said, was at this time at Tupelo, Miss., under malarial conditions, which gave more apprehension than the overshadowing reputation of General Pope, soon to be hailed as the "coming man" and the successor of McClellan. There were no other troops west of the Cumberland range of any consequence, except those already referred to at Vicksburg, and contiguous territory. In East Tennessee, towards which the formidable army of General Buell was about to move, there was a force not larger than that of Gen. G. W. Morgan, soon to occupy its strongest defense. Gen. E. Kirby Smith, a trained soldier, was in command of the department of East Tennessee with headquarters at Knoxville. The force under him consisted only of the two small divisions of Gen. C. L. Stevenson and Gen. D. Leadbetter, with a small but efficient body of cavalry. Gen. G. W. Morgan, of Buell's army, had already moved with his division against Cumberland Gap, and by flanking it through gaps to the south, had reached the valley on the east side, threatening to immure Stevenson in the gap as Morgan was later by the Confederates. General Smith moved from Knoxville to meet Morgan, if he should turn in that direction; but on the 18th Stevenson was compelled to evacuate the gap before Morgan's superior numbers, and the Federals occupied the Gap General Smith, who had been apprised of the Federal movement from Corinth, now realized the full scope of Buell's plan for the occupation of East Tennessee. His situation was so critical that on the 12th of June, prior to the occupation of the Gap, he had applied to General Beauregard for aid, stating that his department was threatened from Cumberland Gap and Middle Tennessee. Beauregard replied that it would be fatal to detach any troops from his army. The situation was indeed alarming. General Morgan had requested General Buell to make a demonstration against Chattanooga, and on the 14th of June a part of Gen. O. M. Mitchel's division had occupied Stevenson, and on the 18th had made a demonstration opposite Chattanooga as if intending to cross. At this time the only force at Chattanooga consisted of a part of Leadbetter's division with no other infantry nearer than that confronting General Morgan at Cumberland Gap. A vigorous movement on Chattanooga would have resulted in its capture, and the consequences would have been very disastrous to the Confederate cause. General Halleck seems to have contemplated that this contingency might arrive, as in a letter to Secretary Stanton of June 12th (Rebellion Records, Vol. XVI, part 2, page 14), he says: "General Buell 's column is moving toward Chattanooga and Cumberland Gap. If the enemy should have evacuated East Tennessee and Cumberland Gap, as reported, Buell will probably move on Atlanta. It will probably take some time to clean out the guerrilla parties in West Tennessee and North Mississippi, and I shall probably be obliged to use hemp pretty freely for that purpose." This Utopian view of the expected millennium when hemp could be substituted for bayonets indicated a very optimistic but erroneous diagnosis of the situation.

On the 17th of June General Beauregard, who had long been an invalid, was given leave of absence to recuperate his health and General Bragg succeeded to the command of the Confederate army at Tupelo, Miss. Of this army the Federal commander in front of it did not seem to have any very high opinion. In fact, he scarcely thought it worth going after, although not more than a day or two's march south of him. He was yearning for bigger game and doubtless looking forward then to meeting General Lee, as he did later in the Second Manassas campaign as the successor of General McClellan, with his headquarters in the saddle. General Pope, whose special province it was to keep his eye on Beauregard, when interrogated by General Halleck as to the truth of a rumor that reinforcements were being sent by Beauregard to Richmond, sent this answer:

Headquarters Army of the Mississippi,
Near Danville, June 12, 1862.

Major-General Halleck:

If any portion of Beauregard's army has left this country, except the numerous deserters who have returned to their homes, the testimony of agents and deserters is worthless. I myself do not doubt that of what is left of his army, two-thirds is now scattered along the road to Columbus for 60 miles in no condition for service anywhere. Beauregard may possibly have 35,000 reliable troops, though I consider that a large estimate, but they are fully occupied in securing his rear, protecting the artillery and supplies and preventing the entire dispersion of the remainder. Without abandoning everything except their arms no considerable portion of them can now be transferred elsewhere. Such at least is my opinion from all the information I can obtain.

JOHN POPE, Major-General.

It is a maxim as sound in war as in peace never to underestimate one's enemy. Yet here was a man deemed fit to command the army of the Potomac, who looked upon the army in front of him as a lot of tatterdemalions, and spoke of them as contemptuously as if they were no more to be feared than a swarm of yellow-jackets. How fatal the mistake! From that very body was soon to form the nucleus of an army which within less than 90 days would force Buell back to the Ohio and yet leave enough to hold the line of Tupelo.

General Bragg, on assuming command, after having considered the possibility of striking General Buell on his right flank as he proceeded eastward through North Alabama, and finding the movement too hazardous on account of the protection afforded by the Tennessee river, adopted the bolder design of transferring the bulk of his army to Chattanooga, and by flanking Buell ere he got to East Tennessee, in conjunction with a similar movement by Kirby Smith, to take possession of Kentucky and force the evacuation of Tennessee, Kentucky and all the territory south of the Ohio river. Having received from Richmond full authority to make the necessary dispositions, on the 27th of June he sent Gen. John P. McCown with his division to Chattanooga via Mobile, who arrived on the 4th of July and assumed command. Then by concert of action with General Smith he began his preparation for transferring to Chattanooga the best part of his army, his scheme requiring his artillery and trains to go by country roads over the rough intervening territory four hundred miles, while his troops would in due season be moved by rail by way of Mobile and Montgomery. In the retrospect it seems impossible that such a movement could be effected without being discovered and thwarted by a vigilant enemy, especially with the means at his command, even discrediting the report of General Pope as to the effete condition in which the Confederate army was said to be. Leaving these preparations to be carried into execution, it is proper to pass in review another agency which had been overlooked by the Federal commanders, and which was to prove such an important factor in the expedition and in the future service of the Confederate army.

CHAPTER IX

CONFEDERATE CAVALRY — THE TWO GREAT LEADERS — JOHN HUNT MORGAN, ORIGINATOR OF THE RAID — SKETCH OF HIS LIFE — HIS ENTRANCE UPON DUTY AND EARLY EXPLOITS — RAPID GROWTH OF HIS COMMAND — HIS DASHING RAIDS — NATHAN BEDFORD FORREST — HIS STRIKING CHARACTERISTICS AND VALUABLE SERVICE — GENERAL BUELL'S EMBARRASSMENTS — HOW HE WAS HARASSED BY THESE TWO COMMANDERS — MORGAN'S FIRST GREAT RAID THROUGH KENTUCKY — HIS FULL REPORTS OF SAME — EFFECT OF HIS BRILLIANT MOVEMENT — THE CONSTERNATION CREATED BY IT — CAPTURE OF MURFREESBORO BY GENERAL FORREST WITH 1,400 PRISONERS — GENERAL BUELL'S COMMENTS ON SAME — HIS MOVEMENTS PARALYZED BY THESE RAIDS — CAPTURE OF GALLATIN, TENN., WITH MANY PRISONERS, BY GENERAL MORGAN — IN BUELL'S REAR — DESTRUCTION OF HIS LINES OF COMMUNICATION — DEFEAT OF BRIGADIER-GENERAL JOHNSON AT HARTSVILLE, AND HIS CAPTURE BY GENERAL MORGAN — MORGAN'S ADDRESS TO HIS COMMAND

UP to this time cavalry had played an unimportant part in the operations of either army. With no reflection upon the merits of other commanders of cavalry, as Forrest and Wheeler in the West and J. E. B. Stuart and Hampton in the East, who afterwards became conspicuous for their great achievements, the man who first demonstrated in the Confederate war the value of cavalry as an adjunct to the infantry, and who above all others was the originator during the war of that system of effective warfare known as the raid, was John H. Morgan. His was not the cavalry known before his time, as the compact, slow-moving, heavily accoutered horsemen, who moved with infantry and were used upon the flank in marches, or in battle to be brought in at the critical moment for an irresistible charge; but the mounted light infantrymen, drilled to fight on foot when necessary and inured to long marches, who did not hover near the infantry for protection, but acting as its advanced scout, could on occasions cut loose from all communications with the base and by great detours get to the rear of the enemy, destroy his lines of communication, burn his bridges and stores, and retard his operations by the diversion of large bodies of men to protect threatened points.

For the service in which Morgan rose to such distinction he was fortunately well adapted by all the conditions calculated to secure success. He was an educated man with some experience in the Mexican war as lieutenant of cavalry, and afterwards, as the captain of a volunteer rifle company, was noted for the discipline and superior drill of his command. Of strikingly handsome features and physique, he had an address which inspired in those associated with him, confidence, respect and friendship. His influence over men was such that if he had selected politics for his field, he could have had advancement at his will. But he chose a more quiet pursuit, and when the war broke out, he was a successful manufacturer, with a lingering taste for tactics which found its expression in being for a number of years at the head of a military company of the young men of Lexington, which was the pride of the town. Like most Kentuckians he was fond of a horse and of outdoor sports, and sat a saddle like a centaur.

Notwithstanding the agitation and excitement which for four or five months had existed in Kentucky at the inception of hostilities and had led numbers of young men to leave their homes for service in the Confederate army, Morgan had not been allured from his customary pursuits. All of his associations, sympathies and interests were Southern, but his temperament was cool, his mind was not inflamed with politics, and like many of the people of his State and locality, he put faith in the asseverations of his Union friends who proclaimed neutrality the panacea for all our ills and the ultimate preserver of peace. He had an abiding faith in the assurance that no one would be molested for his opinions as declared by the resolutions of the legislature, the proclamation of the governor and the general orders of General Anderson when he became the military commander of Kentucky. If he had so desired or intended, he could have taken his company fully equipped away in safety and comfort, yet he remained at home until the process of arrests and the deportation of private citizens to Northern prisons began in violation of all good faith. Suddenly by night his town was invaded by a force from Camp Dick Robinson for the purpose of arresting General Breckinndge and other prominent citizens, who, like himself, had rested secure in the pledges given. Then when it was whispered that he himself was to be a victim, on the next night, September 20th, his resolution was taken, and placing his guns in a wagon with a few of his friends hastily summoned, he eluded the pickets, and mounted made his way to Bowling Green. Reference has been made to his arrival there with 200 men who had joined him singly and in squads, and who attached themselves to various commands in process of organization. With a small body of 20 or 30 men he at once entered upon duty, scouting to the front, and from the beginning displayed the daring which afterwards characterized his operations, passing in rear of the enemy, learning their force and movements and inflicting damage upon bridges, depots and trains. His force gradually increased until it was known as a squadron, with his most trusted men as his lieutenants, and he became of the most valuable aid to the commanding general in the celerity of his movements and the accuracy of his information. When the army fell back through Nashville, he covered its rear and picketed close to the Federal lines.

His first raid was made after General Johnston had started from Murfreesboro for Corinth and Shiloh. On the 7th of March, with Lieutenant-Colonel Wood, ten Texas Rangers and fifteen of his own squadron, he proceeded through by-roads to within eight or ten miles of Nashville, and next morning, in the immediate vicinity of that place, commenced capturing Federal army wagons as they came along, and disarming the men until he had 98 prisoners, including several officers. He then divided his command into three parties and started back with his prisoners, but one detachment was pursued by the Fourth Ohio cavalry and obliged to abandon sixty of the prisoners. Notwithstanding this he brought in 38 prisoners with a large number of horses, mules, pistols, saddles, etc. A second raid was made on the 15th, when he and Colonel Wood with forty men set out from Murfreesboro secretly and in separate parties in the afternoon. They made a rapid night march after reuniting, and reached Gallatin, on the Louisville & Nashville railroad, twenty-six miles north of Nashville, at 4 o'clock p. m. the next day. Here he seized the telegraph office with several of General Buell's dispatches and burned all the rolling stock and water tanks of the railroad, returning with five prisoners and without loss, through the enemy's lines to Shelbyville, Tenn. Gallatin was several times during the war the scene of his most successful raids.

At the battle of Shiloh he rendered valuable service both in the advance and the retreat and on the flank of the army during the battle. Shortly after the battle he received permission to make a dash into Tennessee, and on the 26th of April, with a force of 350 men, composed of his own squadron and detachments from Col. Wirt Adams' regiment and McNairy's battalion, he crossed the Tennessee river on a small horse ferry and on the 30th reached Lawrenceburg, Tenn., where the troops encamped for the night. Next day he attacked and routed 400 convalescents employed in erecting a telegraph line, capturing and paroling many prisoners. He then passed around Nashville and reached Lebanon, about thirty miles east, on the night of May 4th. His command was fatigued by the constant service, and he concluded to rest there until morning; but during the night, which was dark and rainy, he was overtaken by General Dumont, who had left Nashville with the First Kentucky cavalry, Colonel Wolford, and the Twenty-first Kentucky infantry. Morgan's pickets were in a house, and before the alarm could be given Wolford's cavalry charged full upon the camp and came near capturing the whole command. Morgan, with fifteen of his men, escaped, and on the 6th reached Sparta at the foot of the Cumberland mountains, east of Lebanon, where during the next three days fifty of his men joined him. One hundred and twenty-five of his men were captured and six killed. Most of the rest made their way through the Federal lines by circuitous routes and rejoined their several commands. Nothing daunted by this mishap he left Sparta on the 9th with 150 men, mostly recruits, and going in the direction of Bowling Green, entered territory familiar to him, capturing two trains of cars which he burned, and a number of prisoners whom he paroled. About the middle of May he returned to the army at Corinth, and after a short rest began the work of organizing a larger and more effective command with a view of a more extensive raid into Kentucky. Capt. Basil W. Duke, who afterward won distinction scarcely second to that of General Morgan, had been with him from the start as his most trusted lieutenant, but had not been able to accompany him on his last raid on account of a wound received at Corinth, and having collected about 30 of Morgan's men who had been left behind, now rejoined him. Capt. Richard M. Gano, a Kentuckian from Texas, and Capt. John Hoffman from the same State, here also united their two companies of Rangers with the squadron, and its three companies being now recruited to a maximum, General Morgan proceeded to Chattanooga as a better base for his proposed operations. On his arrival there he found three hundred men of the First Kentucky infantry, whose term of service had just expired in Virginia, who at once joined his command, and thus three more companies were organized. The command was then formed into a regiment, with John H. Morgan as colonel; Basil W. Duke, lieutenant-colonel; G. W. Morgan, a Tennesseean and cousin of John H. Morgan, major; Gordon E. Niles, adjutant; David H. Llewellyn, A. Q. M.; Hiram Reese, A. C. S.; Thomas Allen, surgeon; and Dr. Edelin, assistant surgeon. The companies were commanded as follows: Capt. Jacob Cassell, Company A; Capt. John Allen, Company B; Capt. J. W. Bowles, Company C; Capt. John B. Castleman, Company D; Capt. John Hutchinson, Company E; Capt. Thomas B. Webber, Company F; and Captain McFarland, Company G. These six companies and a fragment of the seventh numbered nearly 400 men, and the regiment became known as the Second Kentucky cavalry. The Texas Rangers were made a battalion, with Maj. R. M. Gano in command. They then moved to Knoxville. Some of the regiment, as General Duke in the history* of the command says, were mounted, and the remainder "had hopes;" for it must be borne in mind that in the South cavalry horses were not furnished by the government as in the North. In the latter part of June, Colonel Hunt arrived from Georgia with a company of partisans, which became a part of General Morgan's command, and increased his force to 870, of whom fifty or sixty were unmounted and 250 unarmed at the time he started into Kentucky.

But Morgan did not monopolize the laurels in the field of his special distinction. In the long list of brave and efficient soldiers furnished to the Confederate army by Tennessee, well called the Volunteer State, the name of N. B. Forrest will always stand in her history in the first rank. He, too, was a quiet man, older by some years than Morgan, and without the same advantages of education, but a born soldier, who, with no military knowledge derived from books, knew as much of military strategy as Jomini, could command a division as well as a company and, saber in hand, was as ready to charge a regiment as a squad. Nothing daunted him, and he inspired his men with the magnetism of his own zeal and courage. He was a soldier of conspicuous presence, tall, broad-shouldered, and of strong, handsome features — a man of few words and intense action. He was a citizen of Memphis, and in October, 1861, organized a cavalry regiment of eight

*History of Morgan's Cavalry, by Basil W. Duke, Cincinnati, 1869.

companies, aggregating about 650 men. When General Johnston took command at Bowling Green, Forrest at his own request was assigned to duty with General Lloyd Tilghman, in command at Hopkinsville, and picketed and scouted to the front between there and the Ohio river, covering General Johnston's left wing. The Federals maintained a good force at Henderson, Owensboro and other points along the Ohio to Paducah, and frequent skirmishes occurred between detachments of infantry and cavalry from these points and Colonel Forrest's command. The first regular cavalry engagement in Kentucky took place at Sacramento, between a detachment of Forrest's command led by himself, and one from Col. James S. Jackson's Third Kentucky cavalry, commanded by Maj. Eli H. Murray; in which, though the latter was defeated, he showed so much gallantry that he soon became the youngest brigadier-general in the Federal service. The casualties were few, numbering among them the death of Captain Meriwether, a Confederate, and Capt. Albert S. Bacon, a Federal officer. At Donelson Colonel Forrest won distinction by his services on the left, and in the battle of the 15th he assisted materially in driving back the Federal right wing. He covered the retreat of General Johnston from Murfreesboro and took an active part in the battle of Shiloh and in the subsequent operations about Corinth. When the preparations were set on foot for the expedition to Kentucky, he was sent in advance to Chattanooga, and on the march to Kentucky he covered the right wing of Bragg's army under General Polk. As the details of General Forrest's operations belong to the history of Tennessee, and will be doubtless thoroughly treated in that volume, it has only been deemed necessary to refer to his operations bearing on Kentucky.

General Buell, meanwhile, was encountering many obstacles in his progress eastward through Tennessee and north Alabama. He had to rebuild bridges and repair railroads for the transportation of his army and to open a line of supply with his base on the Ohio. His army was much dispersed, it being necessary to guard his right flank and at the same time to so dispose his force as not to disclose the objective point, for while he had made up his mind to reach east Tennessee via McMinnville and Altamont, he was repairing the railroad and marching a column in the direction of Chattanooga to disconcert the enemy, or to take it if left unoccupied. He was encompassed by difficulties of the extent of which his superiors were but ill acquainted. Besides, he was never a favorite at Washington, and his suggestions and requests were received with scant approval, delayed or grudgingly complied with. He had incurred enmities and awakened jealousies in his own command which afterward bore fruit in his removal from command and prolonged prosecution before a military commission. As to the danger of attack from General Bragg in flank or front, while he appears to have exercised vigilance, he well says in his statement reviewing the evidence before the commission: "I did not anticipate that the enemy was to be left so unemployed at other points that he could direct his great efforts against my enterprise."

Major-General Halleck's western department headquarters had been at Corinth until June 16th, when he retired to Washington to become general-in-chief of the Federal armies. General Rosecrans, who about this time succeeded Pope in command of the army of the Mississippi, became early aware of the transfer of troops eastward by Bragg, and it is unaccountable that his army remained inactive and permitted it to be done. While thus hampered, neglected, and overwhelmed with the magnitude of the work before him and the responsibility of protecting a line of 300 miles from Cumberland Gap to Corinth, Gen. John H. Morgan spread consternation throughout Kentucky and Tennessee by his great raid into the former State. Leaving Knoxville on the 4th of July by way of Kingston and Sparta, he passed rapidly through Tompkinsville, Ky., where he crossed the Cumberland to Glasgow, Lebanon, Harrodsburg, Versailles, Georgetown and Cynthiana, where he had a heavy engagement on the 17th. Thence he returned south via Paris, Winchester, Crab Orchard, Somerset and Sparta, making the great circuit in twenty-five days, capturing many prisoners and destroying much military property and securing valuable recruits. Besides this, great demoralization was caused throughout General Buell's army and department, and many times the number of troops in his command were diverted from other service to protect threatened points or attempt Morgan's capture.

Following are the reports of General Morgan, giving the details of this remarkable raid:

Brigade Headquarters,
Tompkinsville, Ky., July 9, 1862.

Sir: I have the honor to report that I arrived with my command at the Cumberland river and passed the ford about 2 p. m. yesterday, 8th inst. My forces consisted of Colonel Hunt's Georgia regiment of cavalry, my own regiment and a squadron of Texas Rangers. We were joined at the river by two companies under Captains Hamilton and McMillan. I received information that the enemy had passed Cumberland river at Salina the day of my arrival, with about 780 men, but did not deem it right to attack that force, as I was aware that a considerable body of cavalry, about 380 or 400 strong, were stationed at this town, and I thought by a rapid night march I might succeed in surprising them. I left the river at 10 p. m. on the 8th inst., and at 5 a. m. this day I surprised the enemy and having surrounded them, threw four shells into their camp and then carried it by a dashing charge. The enemy fled, leaving 22 dead and 30 or 40 wounded in our hands. We have 30 prisoners and my Texas squadron is still in pursuit of the fugitives. Among the prisoners is Major Jordan, their commander, and two lieutenants. The tents, stores and camp equipage I have destroyed, but a valuable baggage train consisting of some twenty wagons and fifty mules is in my session; also some forty cavalry horses and supplies of sugar, coffee, etc. I did not lose a single man in killed, but I have to regret that Colonel Hunt, while leading a brilliant charge, received a severe wound in the leg which prevents his going on with the command. I also had three members of the Texas squadron wounded but not seriously.

JOHN H. MORGAN, Colonel commanding.

MAJ.-GEN. E. KIRBY SMITH,
Commanding, Knoxville, Tenn.

Headquarters Morgan's Command,
Knoxville, Tenn., July 30, 1862.

General: I have the honor to report that upon the day of the engagement at Tompkinsville, a full report of which I have already sent you, I moved my command (consisting of my own regiment, the Georgia regiment of Partisan rangers, commanded by Col. A. A. Hunt, and Major Gano's squadron, to which were attached two companies of Tennessee cavalry) in the direction of Glasgow, which place I reached at 12 o'clock that night. There were but few troops in the town, who fled at our approach. The commissary stores, clothing, etc., together with a large supply of medical stores found in Glasgow, were burned, and the guns were distributed among my command, about 200 of which were unarmed when I left Knoxville. From Glasgow I proceeded along the main Lexington road to Barren [Green] river, halting for a short time near Cave City, my object being to induce the belief that I intended destroying the railroad bridge between Bowling Green and Woodsonville. I caused wires connecting with the portable battery that

I carried with me to be attached to the telegraph line near Horse Cave and intercepted a number of dispatches. At Barren [Green] river, I detached three companies under Capt. Jack Allen to move forward rapidly and destroy the Salt river bridge, that the troops along the line of the railroad might be prevented from returning to Louisville.

On the following morning I moved on toward Lebanon, distant 35 miles from Barren [Green] river. At 11 o'clock at night I reached the bridge over Rolling Fork six miles from Lebanon. The enemy had received information of my approach from their spies and my advance guard was fired upon at the bridge. After a short fight the force at the bridge was dispersed, and the planks which were torn up having been replaced, the command moved forward to Lebanon. About two miles on a skirmish commenced between two companies I caused to dismount and deploy and a force of the enemy posted upon the road, which was soon ended by its dispersion and capture. Lieut.-Col. A. Y. Johnson, commanding the troops in the town, surrendered and I entered the place. The prisoners taken, in number about sixty-five, were paroled. I took immediate possession of the telegraph and intercepted a dispatch to Colonel Johnson informing him that Colonel Owen with the Sixtieth Indiana regiment had been ordered to his assistance; so I at once dispatched a company of Texas Rangers under Major Gano to destroy the railroad bridge on the Lebanon branch, which he successfully accomplished in time to prevent the arrival of the troops. I burned two long buildings of commissary stores, consisting of upward of 500 sacks of coffee and a large amount of other supplies in bulk, marked for the army at Cumberland Gap. I also destroyed a very large amount of clothing, boots, etc. I burned the hospital buildings, which appeared to have been recently erected and fitted up, together with about 25 wagons and 53 new ambulances. I found in the place a large store of medicines, five thousand stand of arms with accouterments, about two thousand sabers and an immense quantity of ammunition, shell, etc. I distributed the best arms among my command and loaded one wagon with them to be given to recruits that I expected to join me; I also loaded a wagon with ammunition. The remainder of the arms, ammunition and the hospital and medical stores, 1 destroyed

While in Lebanon I ascertained from telegraph dispatches that I intercepted, that the force which had been started from Lebanon Junction to reinforce Lieutenant-Colonel Johnson had met and driven back the force under Capt. Jack Allen, killing one of the men and preventing him from accomplishing the purpose for which he had been detached. I proceeded from Lebanon on the following day through Springfield to Mackville, at which point I was attacked by Home Guards. Two of my men were taken prisoners and one severely wounded. I remained at Mackville that night to recover the prisoners, which I did the next morning. I then left for Harrodsburg, capturing a Federal captain and lieutenant on the road; reached Harrodsburg the 13th at 12:30 o'clock. Found that the Home Guards of all that portion of the country had fled to Lexington; a force was also stationed on the bridge where the Lexington road crossed the Kentucky river. My reception at this place was very encouraging. The whole population turned out and vied with each other as to who should show the most attention. I left Harrodsburg at six o'clock the same evening and moved to Lawrenceburg twenty miles distant, threatening Frankfort in order to draw off the troops from Georgetown. Remained there until the return of my courier from Frankfort, who brought the information that there was a force in Frankfort of 2,000 or 3,000 men, consisting of Home Guards collected from the adjacent counties and a few regular troops. From Lawrenceburg I proceeded to Shryock's Ferry on the Kentucky river, raised the boat which had been sunk, and crossed that evening, reaching Versailles at 7 o'clock. I found this place abandoned by its defenders, who had fled to Lexington; remained there that night and on the next morning marched toward Georgetown. While at Versailles I took about 300 government horses and mules. I passed through Midway on the way to Georgetown and was informed just before reaching the place that a train from Frankfort was due with two regiments of Federals. I tore up the track and posted the howitzers to command it and formed my command along the line of the road, but the train was warned of our presence and returned to Frankfort. Having taken possession of the telegraph office I intercepted a dispatch asking if the road was clear and if it would be safe to start the train from Lexington. I replied to send the train and made preparations to receive it, but it was also turned back and escaped. I reached Georgetown, 12 miles from Lexington, that evening, the 15th. Just before entering the town I was informed that a small force of Home Guards had mustered to oppose us. I sent them word to surrender their arms and they should not be molested, but they fled.

The people of Georgetown also welcomed us with gladness and provided my troops with everything they needed. I remained at Georgetown two days, during which time I sent out a company under Captain McMillin to destroy the track between Midway and Lexington and Midway and Frankfort and to blow up the stone bridge on that road, which he successfully accomplished. Hearing that a company of Home Guards were encamped at Stamping Ground, 13 miles distant, I dispatched a company under Captain Hamilton to break up their encampment, burn the tents and stores, and destroy the guns. This was also accomplished, Captain Hamilton taking fifteen prisoners and all their guns and destroying a large amount of medical and commissary stores. I, also, while at Georgetown, sent Captain Castleman with his company to destroy the railroad bridges between Paris and Lexington and report to me at Winchester. This was done.

Determining to move on Paris with a view of returning and hearing that the place was being rapidly reinforced from Cincinnati, I deemed it of great importance to cut off the communication from that place, while I drew off the troops that were already there by a feint on Lexington. I therefore dispatched a force of two companies toward Lexington with instructions to drive the pickets to the very entrance of the city, while I moved [on the 17th] toward Cynthiana. When I arrived within three miles of this place, I learned that it was defended by a considerable force of infantry, cavalry and artillery. I dispatched the Texas cavalry under Major Gano to enter the town on the right, and the Georgia regiment to cross the river and get in the rear, while I moved my own regiment, with the artillery under the command of Lieut. J. E. Harris, down the Georgetown pike. A severe engagement took place, which lasted about an hour and a half before the enemy were driven into the town and compelled to surrender. I took four hundred and twenty prisoners, including about seventy Home Guards. I regret to mention the loss of eight of my men in killed and 29 wounded. The enemy's loss was 194 in killed and wounded, according to their own account. Their excess in killed and wounded is remarkable, as they fought us from behind stone fences and fired at us from buildings as we passed through town. We captured a very fine twelve-pounder brass piece of artillery, together with a large number of small arms and about three hundred government horses. I found a very large supply of commissary and medical stores, tents, guns and ammunition at this place, which I destroyed. The paroled prisoners were sent under an escort to Falmouth, where they took the train for Cincinnati.

I proceeded the next morning toward Paris and was met on the road by the bearer of a flag of truce, offering the unconditional surrender of the place. I reached Paris at 4 o'clock [18th], remained there that night and started toward Winchester the next morning. As my command was filing out of Paris on the Winchester pike, I discovered a large force of Federals coming toward the town from the direction of Lexington. They countermarched, supposing no doubt that my intention was to get in their rear. This enabled me to bring off my entire command without molestation with the exception of two of my pickets who probably were surprised; reached Winchester that day at 12 o'clock, remained till 4 o'clock when I proceeded toward Richmond. At Winchester I found a number of arms, which were destroyed. I arrived at Richmond at 12 o'clock that night and remained until the next afternoon, when I proceeded to Crab Orchard. I had determined to make a stand at Richmond and await reinforcements, as the whole people seemed ready to rise and join me, but I received information that large bodies of cavalry under Gen. Green Clay Smith and Colonels Wolford, Metcalfe, Munday and Wynkoop were endeavoring to surround me at this place, so I moved [21st] on to Crab Orchard. There I attached my portable battery to the telegraph leading from Stanford to Louisville and learned the exact position of the enemy's forces and directed my movements accordingly.

Leaving Crab Orchard at 11o'clock I arrived [on 22d] at Somerset, distant 28 miles, at sundown. I took possession of the telegraph and countermanded all previous orders that had been given by General Boyle to pursue me, and remained in perfect security all night. I found a very large supply of commissary stores, clothing, blankets, shoes, hats, etc., at this place, which were destroyed. I also found the arms that had been taken from Zollicoffer, together with large quantities of shell and ammunition, all of which were destroyed. I also burned at this place and Crab Orchard, 120 government wagons. From Somerset I proceeded to Monticello and from there to a point between Livingston and Sparta, where my command is now encamped.

I left Knoxville on the 4th day of this month with about 900 men and returned to Livingston on the 28th with nearly 1,200, having been absent just 24 days, during which time I traveled over one thousand miles, captured seventeen towns, destroyed all the government supplies and arms in them, dispersed about 1,500 Home Guards, and paroled nearly 1,200 troops. I lost in killed, wounded and missing, of the number I carried into Kentucky, about 90.

I take great pleasure in testifying to the gallant bravery and efficiency of my whole command. There were individual instances of daring so conspicuous that I must beg the privilege of referring to them. Private Moore, of Louisiana, a member of Company A, of my regiment, particularly distinguished himself by leading a charge which had an important effect in winning the battle. The reports of the regimental commanders which are inclosed, are respectfully referred to for further instances of individtial bravery and efficiency. I feel indebted to all my aides for the promptness with which my orders were executed, and particularly to Col. St. Leger Grenfell for the assistance which his experience afforded me.*

All of which is respectfully submitted.

JOHN H. MORGAN,

Acting Brigadier-General, C. S. Army.

R. A. ALSTON, Asst. Adjt-Gen.

*Col. St. Leger Grenfell was a distinguished British officer who had served in the Crimean war and in India, and having tendered his services to the Confederacy, accompanied General Morgan on this expedition as inspector on his staff. He continued with his command until the close of the war and was conspicuous at all times for his dashing gallantry in leading charges and promoting efficient organization. When the war closed, he was denied terms by the Federal government and imprisoned at Dry Tortugas. In attempting to escape in a boat he was driven to sea by a storm, and never heard of.

The effect of Morgan's raid was far reaching and involved much more than the mere physical results narrated so clearly in his report. It convulsed the whole Federal organization in General Buell's department from Louisville and Cincinnati to Huntsville, Ala., at which latter place General Buell had his headquarters. At the time Morgan was between Glasgow and Lebanon, the military commander of Kentucky, at Louisville, telegraphed General Buell that he had 1,800 men at Munfordville, and next day, July 12, "Morgan has over 1,500 men; his force is increasing. All the rebels in the State will join him if there is not a demonstration of force and power sent in cavalry. The State will be desolated unless this matter is at once attended to. This city is so endangered that I am bound to keep force here. Send me cavalry and other reinforcements. I know more of Kentucky than you can possibly know, and unless it is intended to abandon Kentucky I must have the force." General Buell had already ordered five companies sent from Nashville to Bowling Green and five to Munfordville. He communicated to General Halleck the necessity of five more regiments of cavalry, directed General Boyle to send two regiments and a squadron of cavalry to Mount Sterling and Lexington; notified Gen. Geo. W. Morgan at Cumberland Gap of the danger to his line of supplies and hoped he could send a regiment, and assured General Boyle that although he had not a man to spare from his work, he would at once send more troops to Kentucky. The mayor of Cincinnati, being notified, said he would send 500 men, and the governor of Ohio 1,000 stand of arms, while the governor of Indiana said he would send a regiment. All this telegraphing took place on the 12th.

The scare increased. On the 13th General Boyle telegraphed Capt. Oliver D. Greene, Buell's assistant adjutant-general: "Morgan's force is increasing. The rebels are rising in the counties on the Ohio. The State will be under the domination of Morgan in a few days. He will take Frankfort and Lexington if forces are not sent immediately." Then, the specter growing, he telegraphed General Halleck, "Morgan has invaded Kentucky with 3,000 men, robbed the bank, and is murdering and stealing everywhere. My force is inadequate to drive him out. Can you not send us assistance." The men in buckram had grown into a host. Then he pleads with Stanton to know if Governor Yates of Illinois cannot send a force to Paducah, complains that he has over and over again asked for reinforcements from General Buell and adds that "all the forces in Ohio and Indiana should be sent to Kentucky." President Lincoln responds calmly that General Buell's position is such that he cannot deplete his force; and then he drolly telegraphs General Halleck, then at Tuscumbia, Ala.: "They are having a stampede in Kentucky. Please look to it."

Thus it went on until General Morgan took his leave, and then on the 20th, General Boyle telegraphs Buell, "I do not believe now that he had over 1,000 or 1,200 men." They were again veritable men in buckram. When Morgan is well out of reach, he telegraphs General Buell on the 23d, "I shall issue orders that guerrillas and armed squads are to be shot and not taken prisoners. I shall seize horses of secessionists to mount my men and at proper time require them to pay for Union men's property stolen and destroyed." A few days before he had said, "I shall publish an order forbidding secessionists standing for office." The State election was to be held on the first Monday in August. General Buell responds on the 24th: "I approve of punishing the guilty, but it will not answer to announce the rule of no quarter, even to guerrillas. Neither will it be judicious to levy contributions upon secessionists for opinions alone." General Buell's conservatism was fatal to him. He was pursuing the same policy first inaugurated by him, and the very men who had in the previous autumn guaranteed to Kentuckians exemption from punishment for opinions held were now clamoring for their arrest, punishment and disfranchisement. The era was fast approaching when even Federal soldiers were banished or put in irons for dissenting from the extreme policy, property of non-combatants confiscated, assessments levied, and Confederate soldiers taken from prison and shot without trial or personal charge, for the acts of alleged guerrillas.*

But even before Morgan had ceased to vex the souls of his adversaries, a new cause of consternation occurred in the cap-

*On the 21st of July, 1862, General Boyle issued the following general order:

Headquarters U. S. Forces in Kentucky. General Orders, No. 5.

The following general order is issued to be enforced by military commanders in the district of Kentucky. No person hostile in opinion to the government and desiring its overthrow will be allowed to stand for office in the district of Kentucky. The attempt of such a person to stand for office will be regarded as in itself sufficient evidence of his treasonable intent to warrant his arrest. He who desires the overthrow of the government can seek office under the government only to promote its overthrow. In seeking office he becomes

ture of Murfreesboro by General Forrest, in which he displayed his forte as signally as General Morgan had shown his peculiar genius. On the 13th of July he left Chattanooga with the Texas Rangers of Col. John A. Wharton, and the Second Georgia cavalry of Col. W. J. Lawton, and made a forced march of fifty miles to Altamont, arriving at McMinnville on the night of the 11th. Here he was joined by Col. J. J. Morrison, with a portion of the First Georgia cavalry, two companies of Spiller's battalion under Major Smith, and two companies of Kentuckians under Capts. W. J. Taylor and Waltham, increasing his force to 1,400. Resting until 1 p. m. on the 12th he marched for Murfreesboro, fifty miles, and arrived there at 4:30 a. m. on the 13th, capturing the pickets without firing a gun. The Federal forces were under the command of Gen. T. T. Crittenden, of Indiana, and consisted of portions of the Ninth Michigan infantry, Seventh Pennsylvania cavalry, Third Minnesota infantry and Capt. J. M. Hewett's Kentucky battery. They were in three separate camps. General Forrest at once attacked the first two commands in the town with the Texas Rangers, charging their camp, and holding off the other commands a mile and a quarter distant with the rest of his command. The result, after a feeble resistance, was the capture of the entire Federal force of 1,400 men, whom he carried off to McMinnville after burning a large amount of government stores (General Forrest's report, Records, Vol. XVI, part I, page 810). The First Minnesota did not fire a gun; the commander was dismissed the service. General Buell in general orders, July 21st, says of the affair: "Taking it in all its features, few more disgraceful examples of neglect of duty and lack of good conduct can be found in the history of wars." This was another stunning blow, and intensified the alarm. The force of the Confederates threatening further aggressions was exaggerated, and no one could tell when the next blow would be struck. On the 19th, General

an active traitor if he has never become one otherwise; and is liable both in reason and in law to be treated accordingly. All persons of this description who persist in offering themselves as candidates for office will be arrested and sent to these headquarters.

By command of Brigadier-General Boyle.

JOHN BOYLE, Captain and A. A. G.

On the preceding day, Sunday, General Boyle had issued an order requiring secessionists and suspected persons to give up such arms as they had in their possession.

Boyle, not yet freed of the alarm General Morgan had inspired, telegraphed Secretary Stanton, saying that General Nelson, who had been sent to Murfreesboro after Forrest's incursion, had reported that "30,000 rebels threatened him at that place, and he expects an engagement," when the fact is that General Bragg's army was still at Tupelo and there was not a Confederate regiment within a hundred miles.

The effect of this brilliant success of General Forrest can best be judged by the following extract from General Buell's statement in review of the evidence before the military commission (Records, Vol. XVI, part I, page 35). Referring to the campaign at this period, he says: "Morgan had not yet disappeared from Kentucky after his first inroad when Forrest suddenly appeared at Murfreesboro on the 13th of July, surprised and captured the garrison, consisting of 1,400 men, cavalry, artillery and infantry, forming part of the force which was about to march from that place and Tullahoma to occupy McMinnville, and did serious damage to the railroad. Two other regiments which had been designed for Murfreesboro had been detached and sent into Kentucky on the occasion of Morgan's incursion. The consequence of this disaster was serious. The use of the railroad from Nashville, which had been completed the very day before, and which I was depending on to throw supplies into Stevenson for a forward movement, was set back two weeks; the force of Forrest threatened Nashville itself and the whole line of railroad through Tennessee, and the occupation of McMinnville was delayed two weeks." Thus it will be seen that these two small columns of Generals Morgan and Forrest disconcerted the whole scheme of General Buell's campaign, and delayed his operations much more than two weeks, as further developments will show.

General Nelson's division arrived at McMinnville on the 3d of August, and General Buell was actively engaged in concentrating his army there preparatory to crossing the mountains at Altamont for the invasion of East Tennessee, when General Morgan again appeared on the scene as a disturbing element. On the 10th of August, having moved from Kingston, Tenn., by his favorite route via Sparta, he made his appearance at Gallatin, 26 miles north of Nashville, which had been the scene of his raid in March, and at daylight of the 12th captured Col. W. P. Boone and five companies of the Twenty-eighth Kentucky infantry, who were paroled and sent northward at once. He then moved to the tunnel between Gallatin and Franklin, captured the stockade without a fight, and so effectually destroyed the tunnel, 800 feet long, by burning in it a long train loaded with bacon and other supplies, that it could not be repaired for several months. He then destroyed a bridge between Gallatin and Nashville, and forty cars, and withdrew to Hartsville, thirteen miles east of Gallatin, where he went into camp.

Pending this disaster, General Buell had as a precautionary measure sent Brig.-Gen. Richard W. Johnson, a West Pointer, and regarded as one of the best officers in the service, from McMinnville, August 11th, in the direction of Gallatin. His command consisted of about 700 cavalry, made up of detachments of the Second Indiana, Lieut.-Col. R. R. Stewart; Fifth Kentucky, Major Winfrey; Fourth Kentucky, Captain Chilson, and Seventh Pennsylvania, Colonel Wynkoop. He seems to have made slow progress, as he did not reach the vicinity of Hartsville until the 19th, when he first became aware of General Morgan's whereabouts. In the meantime the latter had moved to Gallatin, and on the 21st, General Johnson advanced from Hartsville to attack Morgan, but when six miles west of Hartsville, he met that officer bent on a similar errand. The result was most disastrous to General Johnson's command, as, after a sharp skirmish and a running fight, he was captured with about 200 of his officers and men and the remainder of his force dispersed in a disorderly flight. Reports of the Federal officers engaged are full of recrimination, one against the other, as to lack of courage and misbehavior on the field. General Johnson says, "I regret to report that the conduct of the officers and men as a general thing was shameful in the lowest degree, and the greater portion of those who escaped will remember that they shamefully abandoned their general on the battlefield, while if they had remained like true and brave men the result of this conflict would have been quite different." General Morgan, in recognition of the gallantry of his command, issued the following proclamation:

Headquarters Morgan's Brigade,
Hartsville, Tenn., August 22, 1862.

Soldiers: Your gallant bearing during the last two days will be not only inscribed in the history of the country, and the annals of this war, but is engraven deeply in my heart. Your zeal and devotion at the attack of the trestle work at Saundersville and of the Edgeville Junction stockade, your heroism during the two hard fights of yesterday, have placed you high on the list of those patriots who are now in arms for our Southern rights.

All communication cut off betwixt Gallatin and Nashville, a body of 300 infantry totally cut up or taken prisoners, the liberation of those kind friends arrested by our revengeful foes for no other reason than their compassionate care of our sick and wounded, would have been laurels sufficient for your brows; but soldiers, the utter annihilation of General Johnson's brigade, composed of 24 picked companies of regulars sent on purpose to take us, raises your reputation as soldiers and strikes fear into the craven hearts of your enemies. General Johnson and his staff, with 200 men taken prisoners, 64 killed and 100 wounded, attest the resistance made and bear testimony to your valor. But our victories have not been achieved without loss. We have to mourn some brave and dear comrades. Their names will remain in our breasts and their fame outlives them. They died in defense of a good cause; they died like gallant soldiers with their front to the foe.

Officers and men, your conduct makes me proud to command you. Fight always as you fought yesterday, and you are invincible.

JOHN H. MORGAN, Colonel, Commanding Cavalry.

By this time the disasters were thickening and General Buell was thoroughly aroused to a realization of the storm which was about to burst upon him, of which these were but the preliminary admonitions. The movements of Gen. Kirby Smith in East Tennessee had caused him on the 16th to send General Nelson to Kentucky to take command there, and to make other important dispositions. General Forrest had meantime been active at and about Lebanon, Tenn., and was in touch with Morgan; but while the latter rested a few days to recuperate for the Kentucky campaign about to open, the former remained in Tennessee to await the advance of the infantry from Chattanooga.

Having endeavored to give a succinct narrative of the general condition of affairs in Kentucky and Tennessee and of the cavalry operations which preceded and in a sense prepared the way for the drama of which it may be said in stage parlance to have been the curtain raiser, attention will now be given to Bragg's campaign in Kentucky.

CHAPTER X

BRAGG'S KENTUCKY CAMPAIGN — ITS CONCEPTION DUE TO GENERAL E. KIRBY SMITH — HIS LETTER TO BRAGG SUGGESTING IT — BRAGG'S PREVIOUS PLAN — HIS CONFERENCE WITH SMITH — TRANSFER OF HIS ARMY FROM TUPELO TO CHATTANOOGA — PLAN OF OPERATIONS — ORGANIZATION OF THE FORCES — BRAGG'S COLUMN — SMITH'S COLUMN — GENERAL SMITH'S BOLD PLAN — ITS SUCCESSFUL EXECUTION — CUMBERLAND GAP TURNED, AND EASTERN KENTUCKY OCCUPIED — SCOTT'S CAVALRY — BATTLE OF RICHMOND — GREAT CONFEDERATE VICTORY — OCCUPATION OF LEXINGTON AND FRANKFORT AND THE COUNTRY EAST OF LOUISVILLE TO THE OHIO RIVER — ENTHUSIASTIC RECEPTION BY THE PEOPLE — AMPLE SUPPLIES — CONFEDERATE RECRUITS

THE publication by the Federal government of the official records of both armies throws much new light upon the military operations of the war. Even the best informed during the progress of a campaign were limited in their knowledge of movements to the immediate horizon of their observation and experience, while to but few were known sufficient facts to enable them to understand and to give an accurate account of a great battle or campaign. But with the volumes of the official records before him, in which have been reproduced with remarkable accuracy and completeness almost every order or report, the impartial searcher after truth is able to comprehend every movement from its inception to its close and to rectify many errors which have crystallized into history. An instance in point is to be found in the matter of the Kentucky campaign. A close study of the record clearly shows that while the execution of it was in the hands of General Bragg, the conception and original plan should be credited to Gen. Edmund Kirby Smith. Long deferred justice to the latter distinguished soldier requires, therefore, a brief statement of the facts upon which this conclusion is based, wholly in the cause of historic truth, and with the most impartial fairness to both officers. As has been already stated, General Bragg had succeeded General Beauregard in command of the Western department on the 17th of June, 1862, while Gen. Kirby Smith was in command of the department of East Tennessee with headquarters at Knoxville. With the occupation of Cumberland Gap by Gen. Geo. W. Morgan a few days after this, and the demonstration made by General Buell on Chattanooga in his behalf, General Smith, becoming convinced of the peril which threatened his department, applied to General Bragg for reinforcements. But General Bragg, having conceived the idea of attacking General Buell in flank in Middle Tennessee, as he was slowly making his way eastward, replied that in view of this proposed movement he needed every man. (See Rebellion Records, part 2, Vol. XVI, page 701.) General Smith on the 24th urged upon the authorities at Richmond the necessity of aid, without which they must elect either to give up Chattanooga or East Tennessee, and General Bragg sent Gen. John P. McCown with a small division to Chattanooga, where he arrived on July 4th. For nearly a month, during which occurred the cavalry operations detailed in the preceding chapter, General Bragg adhered to his purpose of moving northward against General Buell and reaching Nashville by that route.*

Meantime Gen. Kirby Smith organized the cavalry commands of General Morgan and Forrest, and sent them on their raids of his own motion, as well as to retard the progress of Buell until Bragg could so strike him, as to relieve his own department.

On the 17th of July General Bragg ordered Gen. Frank C. Armstrong, his commander of cavalry, to move at once northward toward the Tennessee line, as near as practicable to Decatur, preliminary to his advance against General Buell. On the 19th, General Smith, being again threatened, urged General Bragg to send more reinforcements, to which reply was made that it was impossible as he was confronted by a superior force. Richmond being again appealed to on the 21st, General Bragg issued orders directing General Hardee to proceed with Cheatham's, Withers' and Jones' divisions to Chattanooga by rail via Mobile, the artillery, engineer, pioneer and wagon trains to move thence via Aberdeen and Columbus, Tuscaloosa, Gadsden and Rome, 400 miles. There is no intimation that he intended to send additional

*See letter of Gov. Isham G. Harris, Vol. XVI-I, page 710, dated July 28th, in which he says General Bragg expected to go direct from Tupelo to Nashville.

troops or to go himself until after the following letter from General Smith:*

Headquarters Department of East Tennessee,
Knoxville, Tenn., July 24, 1862.

Gen. Braxton Bragg,

Commanding Army of the Mississippi: General: Buell's movements and preparations indicate a speedy attack on this department. The completion of his arrangements was delayed by the expedition under Colonel Forrest. The expedition was sent with the expectation that it would retard the enemy and give time for your advance. Your telegrams of the 20th and 21st inform me that reinforcements have been sent to this department and of the impossibility of entering Middle Tennessee from your present position. The enemy will, I think, attempt no invasion of Mississippi or Alabama this summer. The character of the country, the climate, and the necessity for concentration East, are insurmountable obstacles; he will confine his efforts to securing his present conquests and to obtaining possession of East Tennessee, making it a base for fall and winter operations. Can you not leave a portion of your forces in observation in Mississippi and shifting the main body to this department, take command in person?

There is yet time for a brilliant summer campaign; you will have a good and secure base, abundant supplies; the Tennessee can be crossed at any point by the aid of steam and ferry boats, and the campaign opened with every prospect of regaining possession of Middle Tennessee and possibly Kentucky.

I will not only co-operate with you, but will cheerfully place my command under you subject to your orders. The force now under my command in this department consists of three divisions. General Stevenson commands the first division composed of one cavalry and four infantry brigades. His command, 9,000 effectives, is well organized, mobilized and in good condition for active service. He is opposed by General Morgan, occupying a strong position near Cumberland Gap, with four brigades estimated at 10,000 effectives. General Heth commands the second division, comprising a legion, one brigade of cavalry and three of infantry, about 6,000 effectives. General McCown reports 3,000 effective men in his division. I have placed him in command of the district of Chattanooga. With General Heth, his command numbers 8,000 or 9,000 effective. This department was organized independent of the army of the West and by orders reports directly to the war department. It was, I presume, a mistake of your adjutant-general, calling upon me

*Idem, p. 734. See also letter from General Beauregard to General Bragg, July 22, 1862, Vol. XVI, II, p. 711.

for weekly reports. I have directed my adjutant-general, however, to make out and send you a copy of the consolidated return. You will find a great disproportion of artillery and cavalry and the regiments very generally new levies, lately ordered to the department.

I am, General, your obedient servant,

E. KIRBY SMITH, Major-General Commanding.

On the 30th of July General Bragg arrived at Chattanooga and was met by General Smith, with whom he had a full conference. Next day he wrote as follows (idem, p. 741):

Headquarters Department No. 2.

Chattanooga, Tenn., August 1, 1862. S. Cooper, Adjutant and Inspector-General,

General: In pursuance of my purpose and plan of operations reported from Tupelo, I reached here on the morning of the 30th ult. The troops are coming on as rapidly as the railways can carry them. Maj.-Gen. E. Kirby Smith met me here yesterday by appointment, and we have arranged measures for mutual support and effective co-operation. As some ten days or two weeks must elapse before my means of transportation will reach here, to such extent as to enable me to take the field with my main force, it has been determined that General Smith shall move at once against General Morgan, in front of Cumberland Gap. Should he be successful and our well-grounded hopes be fulfilled, our entire force will then be thrown into Middle Tennessee, with the finest prospect of cutting off General Buell, should that commander remain in his present position. Should he be reinforced meantime from west of the Tennessee river, so as to cope with us, then Van Dorn and Price can strike and clear West Tennessee of any force that can be left to hold it.

Our cavalry forces thrown out from Tupelo are harassing the enemy in that region, and I trust will hold him in check until we can drive his forces from Middle Tennessee. The feeling in Middle Tennessee and Kentucky is represented by Forrest and Morgan to have become intensely hostile to the enemy, and nothing is wanting but arms and support to bring the people into our ranks, for they have found that neutrality has offered them no protection. Both Buell at Bridgeport and Morgan at Cumberland Gap are now and have been for some days on short rations, owing to the exhaustion of the country and our interruption of the railroads in their rear, which leaves them without adequate means of transportation.

Respectfully, your obedient servant,

BRAXTON BRAGG, General Commanding.

At the time this letter was written, while General Buell was really intending to enter East Tennessee by way of McMinnville and Altamont, he was masking his purpose by throwing a force toward Chattanooga, as if intending to go there. Upon this hypothesis Bragg proposed to march north from Chattanooga and move into Middle Tennessee in the direction of Nashville, via Altamont and McMinnville, and to get into what would be Buell's rear if he was in fact concentrating for a move on Chattanooga. General Buell adopted this theory as to Bragg's intentions, and when he moved, made his dispositions to oppose his passage through the mountains by the proposed route. But as will be seen later, Bragg's plan was altered so as not to take the Altamont route, but to keep on to Sparta.

The mountainous condition of the country through which General Bragg's trains had to come from Tupelo delayed their arrival and the advance of his army full a fortnight longer than he had expected and consumed invaluable time. Meantime he was perfecting his organization. His own force consisted of the following commands:

RIGHT WING, ARMY OF THE MISSISSIPPI
Maj.-Gen. Leonidas Polk, Commanding

CHEATHAM'S DIVISION

First brigade, Brig.-Gen. D. S. Donelson: Eighth Tennessee, Col. W. L. Moore; Fifteenth Tennessee, Col. R. C. Tyler; Sixteenth Tennessee, Col. John H. Savage; Thirty-eighth Tennessee, Col. John C. Carter; Fifty-first Tennessee, Col. John Chester; Carnes' battery, Capt. W. W. Carnes.

Second brigade, Brig.-Gen. A. P. Stewart: Fourth Tennessee, Col. O. F. Strahl; Fifth Tennessee, Col. D. C. Venable; Twenty-fourth Tennessee, Lieut.-Col. H. L. Bratton; Thirty-first Tennessee, Col. E. E. Tansill; Thirty-third Tennessee, Col. W. P. Jones; Stanford's battery, Capt. T. J. Stanford.

Third brigade, Brig.-Gen. George Maney: Forty-first Georgia, Col. C. A. McDaniel; First Tennessee, Col. H. R. Feild; Sixth Tennessee, Col. Geo. C. Porter; Ninth Tennessee, Col. C. S. Hurt; Twenty-seventh Tennessee, Col. A. W. Caldwell; M. Smith's battery, Lieut. W. B. Turner.

Fourth brigade, Brig.-Gen. Preston Smith: Twelfth Tennessee, Col. T. H. Bell; Thirteenth Tennessee, Col. A. J. Vaughan, Jr.; Forty-seventh Tennessee, Col. M. R. Hill; One Hundred and Fifty-fourth Tennessee, Col. E. Fitzgerald; Ninth Texas, Col. W. H. Young;

Sharpshooters, Col. P. T. Allin; S. P. Bankhead's battery, Lieut. W. L. Scott.

WITHERS' DIVISION

First brigade, Brig.-Gen. Frank Gardner: Nineteenth Alabama, Col. Jos. Wheeler; Twenty-second Alabama, Col. Z. C. Deas; Twenty-fifth, Col. J. Q. Loomis; Twenty-sixth, Col. J. G. Coltart; Thirty-ninth, Col. H. D. Clayton; Sharpshooters, Capt. B. C. Yancey; Robertson's battery, Capt. F. H. Robertson.

Second brigade, Brig.-Gen. J. R. Chalmers: Fifth Mississippi, Lieut.-Col. W. L. Sykes; Seventh Mississippi, Col. W. H. Bishop; Ninth Mississippi, Capt. T. H. Lynam; Tenth Mississippi, Lieut-Col. J. G. Bullard; Twenty-ninth Mississippi, Col. E. C. Walthall; Blythe's Mississippi regiment, Lieut.-Col. Jas. Moore; Ketchum's battery, Capt. W. H. Ketchum.

Third brigade, Brig.-Gen. J. K. Jackson: Twenty-fourth Alabama, Col. W. A. Buck; Thirty-second Alabama, Col. Alexander McKinstry; Fifth Georgia, Col. W. T. Black; Eighth Mississippi, Lieut.-Col. A. McNeill; Twenty-seventh Mississippi, Col. T. M. Jones; Burtwell's battery, Capt. J. R. B. Burtwell.

Fourth brigade, Col. A. M. Manigault, Tenth South Carolina infantry: Twenty-eighth Alabama, Lieut-Col. John C. Reid; Thirty-fourth Alabama, Col. J. C. B. Mitchell; First Louisiana, Lieut-Col. F. H. Farrar, Jr.; Tenth South Carolina, Lieut.-Col. Jas. F. Pressley; Nineteenth South Carolina, Col. A. J. Lythgoe; Waters' battery, Capt. David D. Waters.

Abstract of field return of the army of Mississippi, commanded by Gen. Braxton Bragg, August 27, 1862:

RIGHT WING

	Officers	Enlistments	Effective Total	Aggregate Present
Infantry	1,103	12,142		
Cavalry	2	46		
Artillery	28	597	13,557	15,647

Command	Present for Duty.						Effective Total.	Aggregate Present.
	Infantry.		Cavalry.		Artillery.			
	Officers.	Enlisted.	Officers.	Enlisted.	Officers.	Enlisted.		
Right Wing	1,103	12,142	2	46	28	597	13,557	15,647
Left Wing	1,025	11,796	30	353	26	668	13,763	16,237
Grand Total	2,128	23,938	32	399	54	1,265	27,320	31,884

The Left wing, army of the Mississippi, commanded by Maj.-Gen. W. J. Hardee, consisted of the divisions of Gens. S. B. Buckner and Patton Anderson. The first comprised the brigades of Gens. Bushrod R. Johnson, St. John R. Liddell, and S. A. M. Wood. General Anderson's division consisted of the brigades of Gens. D. W. Adams, Thomas M. Jones and J. C. Brown, and Col. Sam Powell.

Maj.-Gen. Kirby Smith's army was organized as follows:

ARMY OF KENTUCKY.

FIRST DIVISION, BRIG.-GEN. C. L. STEVENSON.

Second brigade, Col. James E. Rains:—Fourth Tennessee, Col. J. A. McMurry; Eleventh Tennessee, Col. J. E. Rains; Forty-second Georgia, Col. R. J. Henderson; Third Georgia battalion, Lieut.-Col. M. A. Stovall; Twenty-ninth North Carolina, Col. R. B. Vance; Yeiser's battery, Capt. J. G. Yeiser.

Third brigade, Brig.-Gen. S. M. Barton:—Thirtieth Alabama, Col. C. M. Shelley; Thirty-first Alabama, Col. D. R. Hundley; Fortieth Georgia, Col. A. Johnson; Fifty-second Georgia, Col. W. Boyd; Ninth Georgia battalion, Maj. T. J. Smith; Anderson's battery, Capt. J. W. Anderson.

Fourth brigade, Col. A. W. Reynolds:—Twentieth Alabama, Col. I. W. Garrott; Thirty-sixth Georgia, Col. J. A. Glenn; Thirty-ninth Georgia, Col. J. T. McConnell; Forty-third Georgia, Col. S. Harris; Thirty-ninth North Carolina, Col. D. Coleman; Third Maryland battery, Capt H. B. Latrobe.

Fifth brigade, Col. Thos. H. Taylor:—Twenty-third Alabama, Col. F. K. Beck; Forty-sixth Alabama, Col. M. L. Woods; Third Tennessee, Col. J. C. Vaughn; Thirty-first Tennessee, Col. W. M. Bradford; Fifty-ninth Tennessee, Col. J. B. Cooke; Rhett artillery, Capt. W. H. Burroughs.

SECOND DIVISION.
BRIGADIER-GENERAL HENRY HETH.

First brigade, Brig.-Gen. D. Leadbetter —Forty-third Tennessee, Col. J. W. Gillespie; Thirty-fourth Georgia, Col. J. A. W. Johnson; Fifty-sixth Georgia, Col. E. P Watkins; Forty-third Alabama, Col. A. Gracie, Jr., Jackson's artillery, Capt. G. A. Dure.

Second brigade, Col. W. G. M. Davis :—Sixth Florida, Col. J. J. Finley; Seventh Florida, Col. M. S. Perry; First Florida cavalry, Col. W. G. M. Davis; Marion artillery, Capt. J. M. Martin.

First cavalry brigade, Col. Benj. Allston:—First Tennessee cavalry, Col. H. M. Ashby; Second Tennessee cavalry, Col. J. B. McLinn; Third Tennessee cavalry, Col. J. W. Starnes; First Georgia cavalry, Col. J. J. Morrison; Howitzer battery, First-Lieut G. A. Huwald.

Second cavalry brigade, Col. N. B. Forrest:—First Kentucky cavalry, Lieut.-Col. T. G. Woodward; First Louisiana cavalry, Col. Jno. S. Scott; Eighth Texas cavalry, Col. J. A. Wharton.

On the 9th of August General Bragg added to General Smith's command from his own, the brigades of Generals Cleburne and Preston Smith, forming temporarily a fourth division under Cleburne, and also Gen. T. J. Churchill's division, including the brigades of McCray and McNair, constituting the third division of General Smith's army.

On the 9th, General Smith, in a letter to General Bragg, says that from Buell's present position Sparta would seem to be one of his natural lines into middle Tennessee. He also says that he learns that Gen. Geo. W. Morgan has "nearly a month's supply of provisions. If this be true, the reduction of the place would be a matter of more time than I presume you are willing I should take. As my move to Lexington would effectually invest Morgan and would be attended with other most brilliant results, in my judgment, I suggest my being allowed to take that course, if I find the speedy reduction of the Gap an impracticable thing" (idem, p. 748). General Bragg in his reply next day doubts the advisability of General Smith's moving far into Kentucky while leaving Morgan in his rear until he could engage Buell fully, and says he does not credit the amount of Morgan's supplies and has confidence in his timidity. He adds that it will be a week before he can commence crossing the river, and information he hopes to receive would determine which route he would take, to Nashville or Lexington. Van Dorn and Price, he says, will advance simultaneously with him from Mississippi on West Tennessee, and he hopes they will all meet in Ohio. The feeling of hope and confidence in the success of the expedition was at high water mark with every one.

On the 11th General Smith wrote to President Davis outlining his plan for entering Kentucky, which was substantially that executed by him—that he, with Cleburne's division, would cross the mountains by two routes, moving by Rogers' Gap, while Heth would push on through Big Creek Gap to Barboursville, getting in General Morgan's rear, while Stevenson would threaten him in front. Col. John S. Scott, with nine hundred cavalry, would push on to London, Ky., via Kingston. He says his advance is made in the hope of permanently occupying Kentucky. "It is a bold move, offering brilliant results, but will be accomplished only with hard fighting and must be sustained by constant reinforcements." He trusts that Gen. S. B. Buckner will be sent with his column, as there is not a single Kentuckian of influence or a single Kentucky regiment with the command. On the 13th he addressed his last communication to General Bragg before leaving for the front, saying, "I leave here to-night and will be at Big Creek Gap Friday (16th). On Saturday night I will cross the mountains by Rogers' Gap with four brigades of infantry, 6,000 strong and march directly upon Cumberland Ford. At the same time Heth, with the artillery and subsistence trains and two brigades, moves by Big Creek Gap upon Barboursville and Stevenson moves up and takes position close to the Gap in front. Scott, with 900 cavalry and a battery of mountain howitzers, left Kingston yesterday and should reach London, Ky., Sunday.

It was the most brilliant conception of the war, as bold as Lee's move to Gettysburg, and requiring the dash and nerve of Stonewall Jackson. Besides, it was not a single column; it was four, the failure of either one involving disaster and possible destruction to all. His route was through a mountainous country depleted of supplies by both armies, and covering the territory in which Zollicoffer had lost his life and Crittenden's army had been annihilated; through which also Thomas and Schoepf and Morgan had for a year tried to cover the ground, which he, against a greater force than they had ever encountered, proposed to occupy in a few days. His programme, as sketched above, was carried out with the precision of a chess problem. Col. John S.

Scott, with a force of 869 men, styled the Kirby Smith brigade, composed of the First Louisiana cavalry, Lieut.-Col. Jas. O. Nixon; the First Georgia cavalry, Col. J. J. Morrison, and the Buckner Guards, Captain Garnett, left Kingston on the 13th, moved via Jamestown, Tenn., Monticello and Somerset, Ky., and at 7 o'clock a. m. on the 17th captured London, Ky., taking 111 prisoners and a large number of wagons loaded with quartermaster and commissary stores destined for Cumberland Gap. On the 23d lie attacked Col. Leonidas Metcalfe, of the Seventh Kentucky cavalry, at Big Hill, seventeen miles from Richmond, and routed him with heavy loss, then pursuing the enemy in disorderly flight nearly to Richmond. Meantime General Smith, following the line of operations indicated in his letter to President Davis of the 11th, crossed the Cumberland mountains through Rogers' Gap, with the divisions of Cleburne and Churchill 6,000 strong, and on the 18th reached Barboursville, Ky., while General Heth, conveying the artillery and trains through Big Creek Gap, joined him on the 22d.

Being reinforced by a brigade from Stevenson's division, General Smith advanced from Barboursville towards Richmond on the 27th with 12,000 men, and on the 30th attacked the Federal forces near Richmond,* under Gen. M. D. Manson, of General Nelson's division, estimated by General Smith at 10,000. The principal fighting was done by the Confederates under Cleburne and Churchill, Scott's cavalry having been sent to the rear of Richmond. Upon the final rout of the Federals two miles west of that place, the day closed with the capture of over 4,000 prisoners, including General Manson. General Nelson, who came upon the field about 2 o'clock, after witnessing a panic of his own troops as great as that he saw at Shiloh, escaped capture by taking a by-road. The Confederate loss was about 450 killed and wounded, while that of the Federals was reported at 1,050 killed and wounded, and 4,828 captured, besides the loss of nine field pieces of artillery, 8,000 or 10,000 stand of arms and large quantities of supplies. Colonel Scott pursued the retreating forces, reaching Lexington on September 2d, Frankfort on the 3d and Shelbyville on the 4th. It was one of the most decisive victories of the war, and at one stroke practically caused the evacuation of all Ken-

*See Scott's reports, Rebellion Records, part 2, Vol. XVI, pp. 931-32-33. Also reports of General Nelson, p. 908, Manson and others, pp. 910 et seq.

tucky east of Louisville and south of Cincinnati. On the 2d, General Smith occupied Lexington with a portion of his infantry, sending a small force to Frankfort and General Heth with his division toward Covington. Vast quantities of stores of all kinds, arms, ammunition, wagons, horses and mules came into his possession, and he was received with the greatest enthusiasm by the people, the leading Union men having fled with the legislature to Louisville. The Confederate flag was everywhere displayed, and recruiting camps were at once established in the vicinity of Lexington for the formation of cavalry regiments, by Abraham Buford, D. Howard Smith, R. S. Cluke, D. W. Chenault, J. Russell Butler and others.

CHAPTER XI

BRAGG'S CAMPAIGN IN KENTUCKY — FROM CHATTANOOGA TO MUNFORDVILLE — HIS ADVANCE FROM CHATTANOOGA — BUELL FLANKED — BRAGG AT SPARTA, TENN. — NEWS FROM GENERAL SMITH — ALTERNATIVE ROUTES — ARRIVAL AT GLASGOW— BUELL MOVES TO BOWLING GREEN — CHALMERS' DEFEAT AT MUNFORDVILLE — BRAGG'S ADVANCE TO THAT POINT — ITS SURRENDER WITH 4,000 MEN — INTERESTING CEREMONY — PRISONERS PAROLED — PROCLAMATION OF THANKSGIVING

GENERAL BRAGG was unfortunately detained a week or ten days longer than he had expected when General Smith made his advance, by the non-arrival of his trains and the difficulty of crossing to the north side of the Tennessee. On the 28th his line of march northward was, however, taken up. The Cumberland mountains, after traversing the State of Tennessee in a southwest direction as an elevated plateau twenty miles or more in breadth, is bifurcated at Pikeville, about fifty miles north of Chattanooga, by the Sequatchie river, a small stream with a narrow but fertile valley walled in by the two ranges thus formed, the eastern one known as Walden's ridge, although its proper name is Wallen's ridge. The passage over the latter into the Sequatchie valley was tedious and difficult, but was safely effected, and on the 1st of September General Bragg was with his advance at Pikeville, the head of the valley.

General Buell having been contemplating his invasion of East Tennessee across this valley by way of McMinnville, General Bragg had considered as one of the alternatives of his campaign the feasibility of advancing by the same route directly upon Nashville, or the necessity of engaging Buell in the event he should threaten him on his left flank. But finding that he was not in force nearer than McMinnville, he covered his flank well by cavalry under Wheeler and Forrest, and making strong demonstrations with it toward McMinnville, threw his army forward rapidly to Sparta, at the western base of the Cumberland, about thirty miles northwest of Pikeville. Effecting this movement before his purpose was discovered, he thus flanked McMinnville and was in position to threaten Buell's flank at Nashville or his communication northward. At one time he contemplated the feasibility of marching directly northward for Lexington and Cincinnati to effect a junction with Gen. E. Kirby Smith, of whose victory at Richmond he had received intelligence on the 5th day of September. Various reasons, however, decided him against this route. Much of the way was rugged, the country poor and scant of supplies, and owing to a severe drouth ill supplied with water. To these objections was added the urgent desire of the Tennesseeans, whose governor and leading men accompanied him, that he would secure possession of Nashville by a direct advance upon that place or by maneuvering Buell out of it. Adopting the latter plan he moved from Sparta on the 7th, by the very route indicated in his letter to General Breckinridge August 27th, in the direction of Glasgow, Ky., his right wing crossing the Tennessee at Gainesboro and the left wing at Carthage; and marching upon converging lines, arrived at Glasgow with the former on the 12th and the latter on the 13th.

General Bragg remained at Glasgow until the afternoon of the 15th to rest his troops and replenish subsistence and forage supply, as he had started from Chattanooga with but ten days' rations, which had been depleted before leaving Sparta. He had on his arrival at Glasgow occupied Cave City with the brigades of Generals J. R. Chalmers and J. K. Duncan, thus cutting the railroad between Bowling Green and Louisville. General Buell due west from Glasgow, with six divisions. It was at no time the intention of General Bragg to attack Buell at Bowling Green, as he well knew the strength of that position, and the questions of supply and a base would not have admitted of a siege. His purpose was to move to a junction with Kirby Smith in the direction of Lexington via Lebanon, when he was diverted by an unforeseen occurrence.

General Chalmers, but eleven miles from Munfordville, of his own motion conceived the idea of capturing that position, which was reported to have only a small garrison. But upon attacking it with his own and Duncan's brigades, he found it had been strongly reinforced, and the works being fully manned and served with eight or ten pieces of artillery, he was repulsed with heavy loss on the 14th. Thereupon General Bragg, in order to retrieve the prestige lost by this untoward event, as well as to deprive the enemy of this formidable stronghold, moved out from Glasgow on the afternoon of the 15th, General Hardee's corps to Cave City, and General Polk's upon the Bear Wallow road, which crosses the Green river some distance above Munfordville and is the most direct road toward Lexington. On the morning of the 16th he advanced Hardee's corps to the vicinity of Munfordville and made demonstrations for attack. In the afternoon General Polk's corps appeared on the north side of the river and took such position with his artillery as gave him command of the enemy's works from the rear. General Bragg having been apprised at nightfall of Polk's being in position, summoned the fort by flag to surrender, and after some parley Col. J. T. Wilder came under flag to his headquarters and being satisfied that resistance was useless, articles of capitulation were signed. Under the terms his command was marched out from the works at 8 o'clock on the morning of the 17th, and with due form Colonel Wilder delivered his sword to Gen. S. B. Buckner, who had been delegated to receive it, as this was his native county; and the troops grounded arms near Rowlett's Station, in presence of the Confederate army drawn up in line along the road for the ceremony. They were then marched to the rear, escorted in the direction of Cave City, and paroled. The captured garrison numbered about four thousand, with ten pieces of artillery and a proportionate quantity of ammunition, horses, mules and military stores.*

After an inspection of the captured works, which were on the south side of Green river, General Bragg established his headquarters in Munfordville, on the north side, and issued the following proclamation (copied from the original in possession of the writer):

Headquarters Army of the Mississippi,
Munfordville, Ky., September 17, 1862, General Orders No. 6.

I. The general commanding congratulates his army on the crowning success of their extraordinary campaign which this day has witnessed.

He is most happy and proud to acknowledge his indebtedness to his gallant troops for their patient submission under the privations of an arduous march, and the fortitude with which they have endured its

* For an account of this episode and the battle which preceded it, see Rebellion Records, Vol. XVI, part I, page 1081; Bragg's report, PP- 971, 973; Chalmers' report; and from 961 to 971 inclusive for reports of Colonels Wilder and Dunham and correspondence pending the surrender.

hardships. They have overcome all obstacles without a murmur, even when in the prosecution of seemingly unnecessary labor, and have well sustained by their conduct the unsullied reputation of the army of the Mississippi. With such confidence and support as have been so far exhibited, nearly all things become possible.

The capture of this position with its garrison of 4,000 men, with all their artillery, arms, munitions and stores, without the loss of a man, crowns and completes the separate campaign of this army. We have in conjunction with the army of Kentucky redeemed Tennessee and Kentucky, but our labors are not over. A powerful foe is assembling in our front and we must prepare to strike him a sudden and decisive blow, A short time only can therefore be given for repose when we must resume our march to still more brilliant victories.

II. To-morrow, the 18th of September, having been specially set aside by our President as a day of thanksgiving and prayer to Almighty God for the manifold blessings recently vouchsafed to us and to our cause, the general commanding earnestly recommends to this army to devote the day of rest allotted to them to the observance of this sacred duty. Acknowledging our dependence at all times upon a Merciful Providence, it is meet that we should not only render thanks for the general success of our cause and of this campaign, but should particularly manifest our gratitude for a bloodless victory instead of a success purchased with the destruction of life and property.

BRAXTON BRAGG, General Commanding.

CHAPTER XII

FROM MUNFORDVILLE TO PERRYVILLE — BRAGG'S SITUATION AT MUNFORDVILLE — EMBARRASSING CIRCUMSTANCES CONFRONTING HIM — CRITICISMS ON HIS STRATEGY — A REVIEW OF THE FACTS — DISAPPOINTMENT OF THE ARMY IN THE CHARACTER OF THE COUNTRY AND STATE OF FEELING — ABSENCE OF SUPPLIES — NECESSITY OF PROCURING THEM — HIS MOVEMENT TO BARDSTOWN FOR THIS PURPOSE AND FOR CO-OPERATION WITH GENERAL SMITH — THEIR WIDE SEPARATION — MESSAGES TO SMITH — VISIT TO DANVILLE, LEXINGTON AND FRANKFORT — INAUGURATION OF GOVERNOR HAWES — BUELL'S ARRIVAL IN LOUISVILLE AND UNEXPECTED MOVEMENT — SILL'S FEINT ON FRANKFORT — BRAGG'S SUDDEN EVACUATION OF FRANKFORT — HIS FATAL MISINTERPRETATION OF BUELL'S MOVEMENT — CONCENTRATION OF ARMY DEFECTIVE — MOVEMENTS PRECEDING BATTLE OF PERRYVILLE

THUS far General Bragg's expedition had been a success. He had overcome obstacles of which few unacquainted with the character of the country and the inadequacy of his equipment in transportation and subsistence can form an accurate conception. Without a base, and chiefly dependent upon the country through which he had passed for his supplies, he had marched 200 miles upon the flank of a superbly equipped and veteran army of nearly double his strength and had thrown himself across General Buell's path, with Louisville less than seventy-five miles distant and Buell moving on him from Bowling Green.

The situation and General Bragg's strategy have been the subject of much commentary by military critics as well as by those not expert in the art of war; and their criticism has been unfavorable to him. But how far this is due to his failure to secure success afterward, or to the merits of the argument, cannot be decided. Some argue that he should have turned on General Buell and fought a decisive battle for the State. A knowledge of the topography of the country and of other conditions would not sustain this suggestion. Had he gone out to meet General Buell he would have had a river at his back with banks like a canon and only one ford. It would have been the battle of Fishing Creek reproduced. To fight in front of a defile, or with such a river in the rear, is condemned by the first principles of military strategy and by the common sense of good soldiers, whom it demoralizes. Then again if Buell had declined battle, and retired toward Bowling Green, Bragg could not have followed for the want of subsistence. The region about Munfordville is rough and only moderately productive. For a year previous it had been foraged and exhausted of its surplus, first by the Confederates on the south side and then by the Federals on both sides. On the other hand it would not have been wise to march to Louisville without a junction with Kirby Smith, whose force was scattered watching Gen. Geo. W. Morgan and threatening Cincinnati. He could not communicate in time to effect this speedily. The distance to Lexington was about one hundred and twenty-five miles, with neither telegraphic nor railroad communication. Even courier service was doubtful on account of bushwhacking home guards. He was confronted with a problem requiring prompt solution.

A study of the map will show to the military student, judging by abstract rules, and not by the light of after occurrences, that his movement to Bardstown, where he could obtain immediate supplies, be in position to effect early junction with Kirby Smith for advance upon Louisville, and to connect himself with his new line of communication south, via Cumberland Gap, was the best alternative. He had been delayed by the Munfordville affair nearly a week in his direct movement toward Lexington, and had to make his plans conform to his necessities. That the morale of the army was, notwithstanding the capture of Munfordville, affected by this movement, which had some of the features of retreat, cannot be doubted; for there were, besides, other reasons of disappointment.

The reports which had reached the South represented that the people of Kentucky were eager to welcome an army of deliverance, and would flock with arms to join it. There was a belief that it was a land flowing with milk and honey. While both of these expectations had been fully realized by the army of General Smith, and the intelligence of it received by Bragg's army just before crossing the Tennessee line, their own experience had chilled them. Unfortunately they had traversed half the breadth of the State from north to south and encountered none of the typical rich and abounding soil or sympathetic co-operation pictured in their imagination, and experienced little of the enthusiasm which they had expected. Individual welcome was expressed, but cautiously and free from demonstration, for the Southern element, even in the localities where found in the majority, well knew that upon the coming of the Federal troops they would be persecuted and punished. The sympathy was divided, but in Hart and several contiguous counties the Union sentiment predominated and there had been many Federal troops raised there. There was no unfurling of the Confederate flag and cheering as in the Blue Grass region. Even the ladies, usually fearless of consequences, had learned caution, and if they waved their handkerchiefs, it was generally in a hall shut out from the view of their neighbors and visible only to the troops passing in front. At Bardstown it was somewhat better, but the division of sentiment was sufficient to put a restraint upon the Southern element, while those of Union sympathies did not disguise their sentiments nor fail to express their confidence in speedy aid from the Federal army.

To the reasons already given for the absence of popular enthusiasm along the line of Bragg's march may "be added the fact that there were no Kentucky troops with him, nor any of the political leaders whose presence might have inspired a different feeling. In fact, in summing up the situation, it might as well be stated that it was almost impossible to convince the most ardent Southern sympathizers anywhere in Kentucky that the presence of the army meant permanent occupation instead of merely a raid on a large scale. The writer is aware that in writing so frankly upon a phase which none could understand who did not witness it, and then only one sufficiently well acquainted with the people to comprehend it, he will excite surprise in some and dissent in others; but in undertaking to treat of an historic event of the magnitude of this campaign, it is necessary to its philosophic comprehension that such important factors should not be disregarded even at the expense of a suspension of the narrative.

General Bragg on the 18th of September sent the writer, one of his staff officers, to General Smith at Lexington, informing him of his purpose to move to Bardstown and directing him to send there a train of supplies, and while keeping an eye on Gen.

Geo. W. Morgan, to dispose his forces with a view to early concentration at Bardstown for a movement on Louisville. The messages were delivered within forty-eight hours and immediate steps were taken accordingly. General Bragg, having attempted but failed to draw General Buell to an attack, and knowing that he could reach the Ohio river by a practical route further west, began his movement to Bardstown on the 20th and reached there on the 23rd. After a few days spent there, leaving General Polk in command of the army, he made a tour of inspection through Danville via Springfield and Perryville to Lexington, and thence to Frankfort, where, on October 4th, Hon. Richard Hawes, who had been chosen by the council provisional governor to succeed Gov. George W. Johnson, killed at Shiloh, was inaugurated in form. The greater part of General Smith's army was then in the vicinity of the capital.

In the meantime General Buell, whose army had all arrived at Louisville on the 29th of September, being fully equipped and reinforced by a large body of troops there, moved on the 1st of October in the direction of Bardstown on five roads, the Shelbyville, Taylorsville, Bardstown, Shepherdsville, and Lebanon turnpikes; McCook's corps on the left, Gilbert's in the center and Crittenden's on the right. General Sill's division of McCook's corps marched on the Shelbyville pike, advancing on the 3rd as far as Clay Village, 16 miles from Frankfort, as a feint on the latter place.

General Polk—who had been directed in case of an advance in force to fall back in the direction of Danville, with a view of covering Camp Dick Robinson (renamed by the Confederates Camp Breckinridge), where had been gathered a large quantity of stores—upon being satisfied that General Buell's army was approaching, fell back to Perryville, ten miles equidistant from Harrodsburg and Danville. General Bragg mistook the movement of Sill's division to mean that Frankfort was the objective point of Buell's army, and this was the fatal error of the campaign. Several circumstances tended to mislead him. In the first place it was the direct route to the capital and to Lexington, and the most central point in that division of Kentucky against which a Federal force from Cincinnati also could operate. In the next place, while he could readily get information of Sill's movements, the nature of the other routes taken by General Buell's army forbade the prompt receipt of intelligence as to their line of march. There was no telegraphic communication by which he could be advised, and the movement of each corps was covered by that upon the left, veiling their advance from the ordinary means of observation or communication. General Buell's movement had in fact been made with a promptitude which took Bragg by surprise, and with a judgment which could not have been excelled, for neither of which he received proper credit at the hands of his government. Acting under this misconception of the true situation, General Bragg instructed General Polk to move all his available force via Bloomfield to Frankfort, to strike the enemy, which would have been but one division, in the flank. It was an order from the nature of the roads impractical to execute and, considering the actual situation, altogether unwise. General Polk received the order at Bardstown on the 3rd, but consulting his corps and division commanders, in view of his better information as to Buell's real movements, fell back upon Perryville.

Had General Bragg then, treating Sill's movement as secondary, concentrated his army at Perryville, the history of this campaign thence forward might have been different. He had, however, countermanded his order before he heard from General Polk, and on the 4th, upon the approach of Sill's cavalry, retreated from Frankfort to Versailles. The effect of the sound of the Federal artillery was similar to that of the artillery of Waterloo upon the gay throng at Brussels. The capital was full, not only of soldiers, but of civilians who had come to witness the gubernatorial inauguration and to attend a grand ball that night, the beauty of the Blue Grass having come to grace the occasion. The movement to Versailles began at 4 o'clock p. m. without preliminary warning.

"And there were sudden partings, such as press
The life from out young hearts, and choking sighs
Which ne'er might be repeated; who could guess
If ever more should meet those mutual eyes.
And there was mounting in hot haste; the steed,
The mustering squadron and the clattering car
Went pouring forward with impetuous speed
And swiftly forming in the ranks of war."

General Bragg on the 5th crossed the Kentucky river in the direction of Harrodsburg, where he made his headquarters on the 6th, and disposed his forces with a view to concentration at the point against which should be directed the enemy's greatest force. Unfortunately he did not discern this in time. The presence of Sill's division, which had turned in the direction of Lawrenceburg and Salvisa, led him and some others to believe that one of those points, probably the latter, was aimed at. Another circumstance added to this belief. General Buell, who did not think Bragg would make a stand at Perryville, and was moving toward Danville with a view to flank Bragg and get in his rear, as had been done with him by Bragg, had directed General McCook to move from Bloomfield by way of Mackville and Harrodsburg to Danville, expecting Sill's division to rejoin the corps at Harrodsburg. The appearance of Sill near Lawrenceburg and of McCook at Mackville, where he camped on the night of the 7th, seemed to confirm Bragg in his belief that Buell's objective point was Lexington and induced him to select Salvisa as the point upon which to concentrate his troops, with a view of crossing the Kentucky river near that point and giving Buell battle near Versailles.

Accordingly on the 7th of October Bragg directed General Smith to move his command next day to Versailles, and Cheatham's and Withers' divisions of Polk's corps to follow. Later, however, he suspended these orders, in consequence of notification from Hardee at Perryville that the enemy was in force in his front, and sent General Polk from Harrodsburg to Perryville with Cheatham's division to the support of General Hardee, instructing him to "give the enemy battle immediately, rout him and then move to our support at Versailles." As the order was not issued until 5:40 p. m., it was understood that the attack would be made at daylight, October 8th, and that Bragg would start to Versailles early, and have Polk follow after defeating the Federal force at Perryville. His idea evidently was that neither Crittenden's nor McCook's corps was in supporting distance of Gilbert's corps, and that he could crush that fraction of Buell's army by a sudden attack and then concentrate for a general engagement. But in this he was mistaken, as the official publications show that on the night of the 7th McCook's corps was ordered by General Buell to march from Mackville at 3 a. m. on the

8th for Perryville and form on the left of Gilbert, who was in position facing east about three and a half miles west of Perryville. Had the attack on Gilbert been made as contemplated, it is not improbable that it would have been successful; but even then Bragg would have been beyond the support of Smith, and the force under General Polk would have been little better off than it afterwards proved to be.

CHAPTER XIII

BATTLE OF PERRYVILLE — DELAY IN THE ATTACK — BRAGG HASTENS THERE—STATUS AS HE FOUND IT — TOPOGRAPHY OF THE SURROUNDING COUNTRY — ARRANGEMENT OF LINE OF BATTLE — RELATIVE POSITION OF OPPOSING FORCES — CONFEDERATES ATTACK AND SURPRISE McCOOK'S CORPS — CHEATHAM'S ASSAULT ON RIGHT — McCOOK DRIVEN BACK WITH HEAVY LOSS — SEVERE ENGAGEMENT ON CENTER AND LEFT — CONFEDERATE VICTORY BUT VIRTUAL DEFEAT — GENERAL BUELL UNAWARE OF THE BATTLE UNTIL IN PROGRESS TWO HOURS — BRAGG FALLS BACK TO HARRODSBURG — ARMY CONCENTRATED BUT FAILS TO ATTACK — BEGINNING OF RETREAT FROM KENTUCKY — BRYANTSVILLE — GENERAL HUMPHREY MARSHALL

FOR reasons unnecessary to consider here, but which caused a long and embittered controversy, the attack was not made as expected, and General Bragg, hearing no cannon, went himself to Perryville, where he arrived about 10 o'clock, finding General Polk in line of battle with General Hardee's corps on the right of Perryville, left resting near the academy, and General Cheatham on the left of the town; Chaplin's fork of Salt river which runs through the village from the south, being substantially the line. There had been some skirmishing on the right but no engagement, as it was Buell's policy not to give battle until concentrated.

General Bragg assumed command, and after a brief reconnoissance rearranged the line by transferring General Cheatham's division to the extreme right, and advancing Hardee's corps to the west side of Chaplin's fork. About two and a half miles north of Perryville, Doctor's creek, a small stream from the southwest, empties into Chaplin's fork, and near this junction was Cheatham's right. Upon his right was Wharton's cavalry, while Wheeler's cavalry covered the left wing of the army. In the meantime General McCook, who did not march from Mackville until 5 a. m., had arrived with Rousseau's and Jackson's divisions and made his dispositions as directed, on the west side of Doctor's creek, but with no expectation of an engagement.

Bragg's order of battle was that Cheatham should advance by brigades in echelon across the creek and moving under cover of a wood and natural swells, attack the enemy upon his left flank. General Polk was charged with this movement, which as soon as fairly under way was to be followed by General Hardee with an advance of his line, to take advantage of the confusion which it was supposed General Polk's unexpected attack would cause. Before Cheatham's preparations were completed the enemy opened a very lively cannonade in his direction, but with little effect, owing to the favorable topography of the ground, affording immunity from the fire.

It had been expected that the movement would begin at one o'clock, but it was not until 2 o'clock when General Cheatham's division, moving as on dress parade, moved forward. Sweeping around to the right by somewhat of an oblique movement it dashed across the creek, and it was not long before the roar of musketry told that the work was begun and progressing. Soon the music was taken up by General Hardee's command; the air was filled with the sound of battle, and shot and shell were screaming and exploding all along the line. The west bank of Chaplin's fork is a high bluff, with cedars, and commanded a perfect view of the battlefield. The ground rising by a gentle ascent and consisting of cultivated farms with little timber, a panorama was presented such as is rarely witnessed except on canvas. Cheatham's movement, supplemented by a charge of Wharton's cavalry, had proved a perfect success, taking the enemy by surprise, capturing one or more batteries and doubling up his line in confusion.

In the first onset, Gen. J. S. Jackson, a Kentuckian commanding a division; General Terrill, a cousin of Gen. J. E. B. Stuart; and Col. George Webster, commanding brigades, were killed. General Jackson fell among the guns of a battery which he was apparently directing to check the onslaught. It, however, proved irresistible, and the Federal left was forced back a full mile, with the loss of 400 prisoners, including the staff officers and General McCook's servants, carriage and baggage. By this move our alignment was somewhat broken, there being quite an interval between Cheatham's left and the right of Buckner's division. But advantage was not taken of it, as the contest upon the left and center was severe enough to engage the full attention of the enemy. It was a square stand up, hand-to-hand fight. The batteries and lines of both sides could be seen distinctly except when occasionally obscured by the dense smoke which alternately hung over the scene or was blown off by the western breeze.

The point of most stubborn resistance was in the center, where Rousseau's division was assailed by Buckner's division. There was here a large barn which afforded a vantage ground to the enemy. In the midst of the fiercest contest it was fired by a Confederate shell and soon the flames shot high into the air. The effect seemed favorable for dislodging the opposing force, and a charge with a shout carried the Confederate line several hundred yards farther. In this severe struggle the loss on both sides was heavy, but particularly so on that of the Federals in the Fifteenth Kentucky regiment, Col. Curran Pope being wounded, and Lieut.-Col. Geo. P. Jouett and Maj. W. P. Campbell, killed. The enemy had, pending this engagement in the center, reformed in a strong position in Cheatham's front, and the battle raged along the whole line, which if not continuous, faced in the same direction. But when the center gave way, the whole line recoiled and the Confederates held the entire battlefield.

Yet, while the enemy had retired and no longer replied with his musketry, his artillery, actively plied, indicated that he had not retreated far. On the contrary there were ominous reports of danger on the Lebanon road, and apprehensions arose of being taken in left and rear by a reinforcement from Crittenden's delayed corps, as reports of their approach came in by cavalry. Our advance having placed Perryville in our rear with comparatively no protection, the appearance of an infantry force there would have had a disastrous effect; but fortunately it did not occur. The sun went down in a cloudless sky as red in the autumnal haze and smoke of battle as the blood upon which it had looked, while almost simultaneously the full moon, its counterpart in bloody mien, rose opposite. Still the artillery on both sides kept up their fire. Upon an elevation on our left, which had been won with hard fighting, were placed two of our batteries, which sent forth continuous flames, deepening in their lurid glare as it became darker, until only the sheet of flame without the smoke could be seen, while the air was filled with bursting bombs, and the scream of the shell with lighted fuse, or its unpleasant thud as it struck near, was constantly heard. Gradually the fire slackened; the moon rose higher and lit up the ghastly faces of the dead; and by half past eight, over all was the stillness of death.

The battle was over and both armies were lying on their arms. Tactically it was a Confederate victory, strategically it was a defeat. The loss on both sides was heavy, and it proved not only the largest battle fought during the war on Kentucky soil, but one of the bloodiest of the war. Out of 15,000 of all arms, the Confederate loss was 3,396—510 killed, 2,635 wounded and 251 missing. The total Federal casualties were 4,241—845 killed, 2,851 wounded and 515 missing. General Halleck states that General Buell had at Louisville 100,000 men; but the latter in his report gives his whole force which left Louisville as 58,000, including cavalry and artillery, his three corps being about equal in number, say 18,000 each. The Confederates lost no general officers, but Generals P. R. Cleburne, S. A. M. Wood and John C. Brown, commanding brigades, were wounded. One of the most remarkable features of the battle is that General Buell in his report says he did not know that a battle was being fought until 4:30 o'clock, over two hours after it began.*

About midnight the Confederate army was withdrawn quietly to Perryville, leaving a thin skirmish line which retired later. Early in the morning the trains were put in motion for Harrodsburg, and by noon the whole force had arrived at that place. No demonstration was made by the enemy except some artillery firing at 7:30 a. m., of the 9th, indicating that he was on the alert.

On the same day General Smith's force arrived in Harrodsburg and the army was for the first time concentrated. Every indication pointed to a decisive battle. It was expected that General Buell would advance to the attack, and on the 10th an eligible line of battle was formed awaiting his advance. Bragg then had of all arms an army of 40,000 men, and should have fought. At a distance of two or three miles the Federal army was also in line, to the south of Harrodsburg, both armies facing each other as if ready for the conflict; but neither advanced, a heavy rain supervening. General Buell had swung around and occupied Danville, and Bragg, fearing that he would seize upon his depot of supplies at Bryantsville, twelve or fourteen miles east of Harrodsburg, or cut off his communications with Cumberland Gap, instead of following him marched for Bryantsville on the morning of the 11th, and by the time he reached that point the enemy occupied Harrodsburg.

*General Buell's statement in review of the evidence before the Military Commission. Rebellion Records, Vol. XVI, Part I, page 51. General McCook's testimony, Ib., page 90.

The retreat from Kentucky had virtually begun. A council of war was held at Bryantsville. Added to his own condition as the result of Perryville, came news of the defeat of Price and Van Dorn by Rosecrans at Corinth on the 3rd, which shattered the only army in the lower South and left a victorious enemy free to move at will in any direction. In view of this situation, the council with one exception, concurred in the propriety of a retreat through Cumberland Gap while the route was open and the roads were yet good. Gen. Humphrey Marshall, who simultaneously with General Bragg's advance into Kentucky had come through Pound Gap from southwestern Virginia, with several thousand cavalry, favored crossing to the north side of the Kentucky river, sustaining the army in the Blue Grass region as long as possible and then retreating into Virginia by way of Pound Gap. General Bragg so far acceded to his proposition as to permit his return the same way.

And so it was resolved to evacuate Kentucky. Cumberland Gap had been abandoned on September 17th by Gen. Geo. W. Morgan, who had made his way through the mountains by way of Manchester, Beattyville and West Liberty to Greenup on the Ohio, where he had arrived on the 3rd of October. His progress was impeded somewhat by the cavalry of General Marshall and Col. John H. Morgan, but the nature of the country not being favorable for cavalry operations, their resistance availed but little beyond preventing his movement westward, had he so designed. On September 27th a portion of Morgan's cavalry under Col. Basil W. Duke, aiming to cross the Ohio at Augusta for a demonstration against Cincinnati, had a severe engagement in the streets of that town with the home guards, who fired from the houses, causing a loss of twenty per cent of his force, with a much heavier loss to the enemy. Among his killed were Capts. Samuel D. Morgan (a cousin of Col. John H. Morgan), Allen and Kennett, and Lieuts. Greenbury Roberts, George White, Rogers, King and William Courtland Prentice, son of George D. Prentice, editor of the Louisville Journal. This was the only engagement which occurred on the Ohio during the campaign, although previously Col. R. M. Gano, of Morgan's cavalry, had captured Maysville without a fight.

CHAPTER XIV

MOVEMENT IN RETREAT BY TWO LINES — SUCCESSFUL EVASION OF BUELL'S PURSUING ARMY — CRITICAL SITUATION OF GENERAL SMITH'S COLUMN AT BIG HILL — BUELL DRAWS OFF FROM PURSUIT AND PREPARES TO RETURN TO NASHVILLE — CONFEDERATE FORCES REUNITE AT LONDON AND PASS SAFELY THROUGH CUMBERLAND GAP — BRECKINRIDGE WITH HIS KENTUCKIANS TURNED BACK AND SENT TO MURFREESBORO — GENERAL BUELL CONGRATULATED BY GENERAL HALLECK, AND DIRECTED TO TAKE EAST TENNESSEE — IS SUPERSEDED BY GENERAL ROSECRANS — DEATH OF GENERAL WILLIAM NELSON — CONDITION OF KENTUCKY AFTER EVACUATION OF THE STATE — INCREASED PERSECUTION OF SOUTHERN PEOPLE

THE dispositions for the retreat were soon made, and on the morning of October 13th the movement began, General Polk's and General Hardee's corps moving by way of Lancaster, Crab Orchard and Mount Vernon, and General Smith's column by way of Lancaster and Big Hill to London, where he reunited with General Bragg. The pursuit of General Bragg's column was pressed with vigor by General Buell as far as Mount Vernon; but the retreat was so well covered by Wheeler's cavalry that it was without results. Fortunately General Smith was not vigorously pressed, or he could scarcely have saved his artillery and trains, which were carried over Big Hill only with the greatest difficulty, requiring the assistance of the infantry for several days. Col. John H. Morgan lingered in the vicinity of Lexington, covering approaches from that direction, and finally retired with a large increase of his force from recruits, in the direction of Lebanon and Nashville.

The retreat of General Bragg was conducted without further incident, the roads and weather fortunately being favorable, and on the 20th the advance of the army passed through Cumberland Gap. Yet it was an arduous retreat. The change from a country of plenty, with high hopes of wintering in Kentucky, to hard marches with scant food and disappointed expectations, had a telling effect upon the troops, who left the State footsore and poorly clad and shod to encounter a severe snow storm upon entering East Tennessee. Gen. John C. Breckinridge, having been turned back on the 17th when nearing Cumberland Gap, as already related, had moved into Middle Tennessee, and on the 28th of October arrived at Murfreesboro with 2,000 men as the advance guard of the army of occupation, soon to be reinforced by the greater part of General Bragg's army.

General Buell, unable to cut off Bragg's retreat, issued orders looking to the return of his army to Nashville. General Halleck, upon receipt of the announcement of the battle of Perryville and Bragg's retreat, on the 18th of October replied: "The rapid march of your army from Louisville and your victory at Perryville have given great satisfaction to the government," these being the first words of commendation Buell had received since he left Corinth. A number of official communications had been addressed to him in this interval, warning him that he would be removed if he did not show better results, and on his arrival at Louisville he had been met with orders to turn over his command to General Thomas, but the latter protested that this was unjust and the order was rescinded, Thomas accompanying Buell on the Perryville campaign as second in command.

In the same dispatch of congratulation quoted above, Halleck informed General Buell that he was expected to drive the enemy from East Tennessee as well as Kentucky. To this Buell replied that it was impossible to invade East Tennessee at that time on account of the barren country, the approach of winter and bad roads; besides that, a prompt return to Nashville was necessary in order to hold any part of Tennessee. On the 19th Halleck telegraphed: "I am directed by the President to say that your army must enter East Tennessee this fall and that it ought to move there while the roads are passable." Buell, however, continued the movement of his army toward Nashville, and on the 23d General Rosecrans, at Corinth, Miss., was directed to repair to Cincinnati to receive orders. Upon his arrival there on the 28th, he received notification of his appointment to the department of the Cumberland, being the State of Tennessee east of the Tennessee river and the parts of north Alabama and Georgia in possession of the United States troops. He was directed to exhibit this instruction to General Buell and assume command of his forces. On the 30th General Rosecrans presented his credentials to General Buell at Louisville, together with instructions to the latter from General Halleck to repair to Indianapolis and await further orders. These further orders when received notified General Buell that a commission would sit on the 27th of November to investigate the operations of his command. And thus upon the pretext of his not having moved to carry out an order which was not repeated to his successor, General Buell was retired as the culmination of a long antagonism on political grounds, or jealousy on the part of his subordinates and disfavor of his superiors. Among other Federal losses in this campaign was the death of General Nelson, who was killed in a personal encounter in the Gait House, Louisville, September 29th, by Gen. Jeff. C. Davis, of the Federal army. Kentucky, again secure in the occupation of the Federal troops, passed into a new and more complete state of subjugation. Not only were those who had shown their sympathy for the Confederates during their occupation made to feel the hand of power, but soon Union men who ventured to dissent from the extreme policy of the administration were treated as rebels and subjected to equal indignity. The most radical and revolutionary element obtained control, and a reign of terror was soon inaugurated which, subsequently continued through the war under Burnside, Burbridge, Payne and Palmer, not only intensified the Southern sympathy, but finally alienated a large majority of those who had originally been the most pronounced Unionists. But it was too late to be of practical benefit to the cause of the South, and save with an occasional cavalry raid, the soil of Kentucky did not again feel the tread of the contending armies.

CHAPTER XV

RAPID RECUPERATION OF THE ARMY AFTER ITS RETURN PROM KENTUCKY — OCCUPATION OF MIDDLE TENNESSEE — REORGANIZATION OF KENTUCKY TROOPS — THE KENTUCKY BRIGADE AGAIN REUNITED — GENERAL HANSON IN COMMAND — CAVALRY ORGANIZATIONS — BRILLIANT MOVEMENT OF GENERAL MORGAN — CAPTURE OF HARTSVILLE WITH 2,000 PRISONERS — BATTLE OF MURFREESBORO — BRAGG'S ORDER OF BATTLE — SOME DETAILS OF THE BLOODY ENGAGEMENT — SECOND BATTLE — HEAVY LOSS IN BRECKINRIDGE'S DIVISION — DEATH OF GENERAL HANSON — BRECKINRIDGE'S REPORT — RETREAT FROM MURFREESBORO

NOTWITHSTANDING the disappointment which the Kentucky infantry had experienced in not being permitted to take part in the campaign, and the cavalry had suffered in seeing the State abandoned to the enemy, there was no useless repining, but in common with the great body of the Confederate army, cheerfulness was soon restored; and with that remarkable spirit of recuperation which so often manifested itself in the Confederacy after disaster, it was not long before the army had resumed a hopeful and aggressive tone. Although the result of the summer campaign had not brought the fruition expected, the present condition, when contrasted with that which had existed during the spring and summer, was so much better, that there was prevalent more feeling of congratulation at the vantage gained than of repining over that which had not been secured. The Kentucky cavalry had been increased, and on the first of November, 1862, Morgan's cavalry brigade, then in east Tennessee, showed the following organization: Second Kentucky, Col. B. W. Duke; Seventh Kentucky, Col. R. M. Gano; Eighth Kentucky, Col. R. S. Cluke; Eleventh Kentucky, Col. D. W. Chenault; Ninth Kentucky battalion, Maj. W. C. P. Breckinridge; Howitzer battery, Captain Arnett. The Ninth battalion, united with Stoner's battalion, was later raised to a regiment, and its commander became a colonel.

The Seventh, Eighth and Ninth regiments had been recruited during the late campaign in Kentucky, and another, the First Kentucky regiment, recruited and reorganized by Col. J. Russell Butler, was temporarily assigned to Colonel Scott's brigade. A number of other inchoate regiments came out, which, if the occupation of Kentucky had lasted awhile longer, would have all been filled; but as it was, those under Col. D. Howard Smith, the Fifth; Col. J. Warren Grigsby, Sixth, and Col. Adam R. Johnson, Tenth, were soon available and made valuable accessions to the command a little later in middle Tennessee. With General Marshall also went out of Kentucky into Virginia a number of organizations, some of them regiments and others battalions, which did valuable service during the remainder of the war. Among these were the Fifth infantry, Gen. John S. Williams' original regiment, whose time had expired, but which was recruited and reorganized by Col. Hiram Hawkins; the Fourth Kentucky cavalry, Col. Henry L. Giltner; Eleventh Kentucky mounted infantry, known also as the Thirteenth regiment Kentucky cavalry, Col. Benjamin E. Caudill; Second battalion Kentucky cavalry, Maj. Clarence J. Prentice; Second Kentucky mounted rifles, Lieut.-Col. Thomas Johnson; and the Third battalion Kentucky mounted rifles, Lieut.-Col. Ezekiel F. Clay; together with several independent companies of scouts and partisan rangers. While there was recruited no infantry, the various old organizations received accessions from among the many who came out of Kentucky with the army in its retreat, or from proposed cavalry organizations which were disbanded. The Fort Donelson prisoners of the Second and Eighth regiments had been exchanged during the summer, the sick and absentees had rejoined their commands, and the regiments showed well-filled ranks, with a clean bill of health and fine morale. The Seventh, Col. Edward Crossland; the Third, Col. A. P. Thompson; and the Eighth, Col. H. B. Lyon, were in General Van Dorn's army, and had received special mention for gallantry in the late campaign in Mississippi. The Second, Fourth, Sixth and Ninth, constituting the Orphan brigade, were now with General Breckinridge at Murfreesboro.

General Bragg, after a brief visit to Richmond, proceeded to Tullahoma, Tenn., and pushed forward the reconstruction of railroad bridges and the transfer of his army to Middle Tennessee, and by the middle of November it was organized as follows: First corps, commanded by Lieutenant-General Polk, consisting of Cheatham's, Withers' and Breckinridge's divisions; Second corps, commanded by Lieut.-Gen. W. J. Hardee, consisting of Buckner's and Patton Anderson's divisions.

General Breckinridge's division was composed of five brigades: Hanson's, Preston's, Adams', Palmer's and Jackson's, the first three commanders being natives of Kentucky. Hanson's brigade was as follows: First brigade, Col. Roger W. Hanson:—Forty-first Alabama, Col. M. L. Stansil; Second Kentucky, Maj. J. W. Hewitt; Fourth Kentucky, Col. R. P. Trabue; Sixth Kentucky, Col. J. H. Lewis; Ninth Kentucky, Col. T. H. Hunt; Cobb's Kentucky battery, Capt. Robert Cobb, Graves' Kentucky battery, Capt. J. J. Ingram; Kentucky cavalry company, Capt. R. E. Roberts.

General Buckner's division consisted of four brigades, commanded by Generals Liddell, Cleburne, Bushrod R. Johnson and Wood. Of the cavalry is given as among independent organizations, "One brigade of 2,500 men, Col. John H. Morgan commanding, to act as partisans." One of General Bragg's first acts after reaching Tennessee was to recommend the promotion of Colonels Hanson, Hunt and Morgan to the rank of brigadier. In his letter of November 22d to Adjutant-General Cooper, he says: "Col. John H. Morgan is peculiarly suited for the special service in which I propose to employ him—partisan war on the enemy's lines in Kentucky. He has raised his command, and nearly armed and equipped it from the enemy's stores." Later a brigade of cavalry was organized under Gen. Abram Buford, of Kentucky, which operated about Murfreesboro until after the battle, when General Buford was transferred to the Mississippi department. General Buckner did not continue long in Tennessee, but was assigned to the command of Mobile, where he remained until the following spring, when he relieved Gen. Kirby Smith as commander of the department of East Tennessee, the latter being transferred to the Trans-Mississippi.

The army spent the month of December, 1862, before Murfreesboro, drilling and perfecting itself in organization in contemplation of an early attack by Rosecrans, who was collecting a formidable army at Nashville. General Wheeler's cavalry was in front, while Forrest covered the left flank in front of Columbia, where Van Dorn was in command of a force chiefly of cavalry. In the early part of the month one of the most brililiant events of the year took place in the capture of Hartsville, Tenn. The expedition was planned and led by General Morgan and was composed entirely of Kentucky troops: 1,400 cavalry under Col. Basil W. Duke; the Second and Ninth Kentucky infantry, commanded by Col. Thomas H. Hunt; Captain Cobb's battery, and two howitzers and two Ellsworth guns of the cavalry. General Morgan had learned that Federal detachments were stationed at Gallatin, Castalian Springs and Hartsville, his old stamping-ground, and he proposed to repeat some of his exploits of the past summer. Leaving Murfreesboro on the 5th, the command moved to Baird's Mills, half way to Hartsville, which was fifty miles distant from Murfreesboro. It was bitter cold and the ground covered with snow. Here they remained until 6 p. m. on the 6th, when, by a night march, they crossed the Cumberland river five miles below Hartsville by daylight, and shortly after sunrise were in position before that place. It had been expected to surprise the garrison, but this was frustrated by the difficulty of crossing the river, and General Morgan found the enemy fully prepared to meet him. A brisk fight ensued, in which the infantry and cavalry took part chiefly dismounted, while a part of the cavalry mounted was employed in guarding against surprise, as there was another Federal force of eight thousand within five miles. After a sharp engagement of an hour or more, in which the Federal troops behaved much better than in their previous affairs, and in which the Second Kentucky suffered a loss of sixty-two in killed and wounded, the Federal force, numbering about 2,000, surrendered at discretion. There were three regiments of infantry and one of cavalry, all of which, with their arms, wagons and stores, and two pieces of artillery, were carried off to Murfreesboro in safety. The total infantry loss was eighteen killed and seventy-one wounded. The casualties in the cavalry were limited to a few wounded. The event added to the prestige of the Kentucky troops, which was already high in discipline, drill and soldierly bearing.

The battle of Murfreesboro occurred on Wednesday, December 31, 1862. The army, cheered by the Hartsville victory, the good rations afforded by the rich country around Murfreesboro and the enthusiastic devotion of the citizens, was in fine spirits. President Davis had paid them a visit but a short time before, and in a review their splendid appearance had excited his admiration and elicited his warmest praise. Rosecrans gave evidence of his purpose to move nearly a week before the battle, full reports of his force and the location of his several corps being received daily. On the 27th, General Bragg, having selected his line of defense and plan of battle, issued a private circular for general and staff officers, an original copy of which is in possession of the writer, and which is here given, as it has not been found among the published records:

MEMORANDA FOR GENERAL AND STAFF OFFICERS:

1. The line of battle will be in front of Murfreesboro, half the army—left wing in front of Stone's river, right wing in rear of river.

2. Polk's corps will form left wing—Hardee's corps, right wing.

3. Withers' division will form first line in Polk's corps; Cheatham's the second line; Breckinridge's division will form first line Hardee's corps, Cleburne's division second line Hardee's corps.

4. McCown's division to form reserve opposite center on high ground in rear of Cheatham's present quarters.

5. Jackson's brigade, reserve to the right flank, to report to Lieutenant-General Hardee.

6. The two lines to be from 800 to 1,000 yards apart, according to the ground.

7. Chiefs of artillery to pay special attention to posting of batteries and to supervise their work, and see that they do not causelessly waste their ammunition.

8. Cavalry to fall back gradually before enemy, reporting by couriers every hour. When near our line, Wheeler will move to right and Wharton to the left to cover and protect our flanks and report movements of the enemy Pegram to fall to the rear and report to the general commanding as reserve.

9. To-night if the enemy has gained his position in our front ready for action, Wheeler and Wharton with their whole commands will make a night march to the right and left, turn the enemy's flanks, gain his rear and vigorously assail his trains and rear guards, blocking the roads and impeding his movements in every way, holding themselves ready to assail his retreating forces.

10. All quartermasters, commissaries and ordnance officers will remain at their proper posts discharging their appropriate duties. Supplies and baggage should be ready packed for a move forward or backward as the result of the day may require, and the trains should be in position out of danger, teamsters all present and quartermasters in charge.

11. Should we be compelled to retire, Polk's corps will move on the Shelbyville, and Hardee's on Manchester pike, trains in front, cavalry in rear.

(Signed) BRAXTON BRAGG, General Commanding. Sunday morning, Official, GEO. G. GARNER, A. A. G.

General Rosecrans had moved out from Nashville on the 26th, but it was not until the afternoon of the 29th that Wheeler withdrew from his front and he arrived opposite our left wing. It was hoped and expected that he would attack, but he merely showed a disposition to extend his right beyond our left, causing McCown's division to be moved to Polk's left. The 30th was a cloudy, forbidding day, with rain at intervals, and a general engagement was expected, but the enemy refrained from attack and continued to extend his right, threatening to cut us off from the Shelbyville pike. As the troops had been in line three days and nights, General Bragg determined to attack on the morning of the 31st. With that view Cleburne's (late Buckner's) division was moved on the night of the 30th to the extreme left, General Hardee accompanying with instructions to open the fight at daylight, the action to be taken up by the troops on the right.

It was a clear, frosty morning, the last day of the year. Hardee moved into action as directed, and with the first light of the sun the heavy fire of musketry told that he was at work, while its decreasing sound indicated that he was driving the enemy. The movement was a counter-part of Cheatham's attack at Perryville, on the left instead of the right. Polk's corps had its right resting on Stone's river* with its left swung out in alternate fields and cedar brakes upon ground nearly level. Cleburne had struck Gen. A. D. McCook's corps, the same which suffered so from Cheatham's assault at Perryville, while the men were at breakfast, and driven them in confusion, capturing a number of prisoners, including Brigadier-General Willich, killing General Sill, and again capturing General McCook's headquarters with his official and private effects. The battle, taken up by the commands on the right, moved on a right wheel as the enemy fell back, with Polk's right as a pivot, until the line, like the minute hand of a clock, had described a fourth of a circle, halting when it was at somewhat more than right angles to its first position. This halt was caused by Rosecrans' routed line making a stand in a railroad cut, which happened conveniently in their line of retreat, sustained by reserves and heavy batteries in their rear. By noon the battlefield was comparatively silent. Jackson's and Adams', and later Gen. William Preston's and Palmer's brigades were brought over from Breckinridge's line and an attempt made to carry the cut, but the position was too strong, and they were

*This river, which is erroneously called by the Federals Stone river, was named from Uriah Stone, who, in company with James Smith, Joshua Horton and William Baker, explored that region in 1766. "An account of the remarkable occurrences in the life and travels of Col. James Smith, etc., written by himself, Lexington, Ky., printed by John Bradford, Main street, 1799."

compelled to desist after serious loss, Gen. D. W. Adams being severely wounded. General Breckinridge was in command of this attack, the losses in which were heavier than at Perryville. This in brief was the battle of Murfreesboro.

General Rosecrans' alignment was now somewhat the two sides of an isosceles triangle, with the railroad cut for one side, and Stone's river, with its rocky banks unfordable except at good intervals, for the other, and with its acute angle pointing to our center. He was thus unassailable on either flank, and the two armies lay in this position the remainder of the day. At night Wheeler made a circuit to the rear of Rosecrans' army, destroying many wagons and harassing him in every possible manner. He was known to have been crippled, and on the morning of the 1st, of January was reported to be retreating. A reconnoissance in force with infantry and artillery proved to the contrary, however, and the day wore away without other movement.

On Friday, the 2d, it was evident that Rosecrans was holding on with dogged persistence, and the tension upon the Confederate troops, who had to keep constant vigil in advanced lines where they could have little if any fire, and remote from their supplies, was telling visibly. Up to this time the enemy had made but little demonstration upon our right held by Breckinridge, where the ground was more undulatory than on the left, but the morning developed the fact that they had crossed some troops to the east bank, with evidence of an effort to extend their line beyond our right as had been tried on the left. This brought on the disastrous battle so fatal to the Kentuckians and the right wing. At two o'clock, after a conference of corps and some division commanders at the ford which marked our center, General Bragg directed General Breckinridge in person to dislodge the enemy from the position he had taken on an eminence in his front. Much controversy and feeling ensued over this order afterwards, General Bragg contending that his directions were to dislodge the enemy but not to pursue him, or bring on an engagement. It was a fair, mild afternoon, about 4 o'clock, when the movement was made. As this was the first great battle in which the Kentucky brigade had been engaged since Shiloh, it is deemed best to give General Breckinridge's report of it, being part of his general report of the operations of his command covering the several preceding days:

"On Friday, the 2nd of January, being desirous to ascertain if the enemy was establishing himself on the east bank of the river, Lieut.-Col. John A. Buckner and Maj. Rice E. Graves, with Captain Byrne's battery and a portion of the Washington artillery, under Lieutenant Vaught, went forward to our line of skirmishers, to the right, and engaged those of the enemy, who had advanced perhaps a thousand yards from the east bank of the river. They soon revealed a strong line of skirmishers, which was driven back a considerable distance by our sharpshooters and artillery, the latter firing several houses in the fields in which the enemy had taken shelter. At the same time, accompanied by Maj. Wm. D. Pickett of Lieutenant-General Hardee's staff and by Maj. James Wilson, Col. Theodore O'Hara and Lieut. J. Cabell Breckinridge, of my own, I proceeded toward the left of our line of skirmishers, which passed through a thick wood about five hundred yards in front of Hanson's position and extended to the river. Directing Captain Bosche of the Ninth and Captain Steele of the Fourth Kentucky to drive back the enemy's skirmishers, we were enabled to see that he was occupying with infantry and artillery the crest of a gentle slope on the east bank of the river. The course of the crest formed a little less than a right angle with Hanson's line, from which the center of the position I was afterward ordered to attack was distant about sixteen hundred yards. It extended along ground part open and part woodlands.

"While we were endeavoring to ascertain the force of the enemy and the relation of ground on the east bank to that on the west of the river, I received an order from the commanding general to report to him in person. I found him on the west bank near the ford below the bridge, and received from him an order to form my division in two lines and take the crest I have just described with the infantry. After doing this I was to bring up the artillery and establish it on the crest, so as to at once hold it and enfilade the enemy's lines on the other side of the river. Pegram and Wharton, who, with some cavalry and a battery were beyond the point where my right would rest, when the new line of battle should be formed, were directed, as the general informed me, to protect my right and co-operate in the attack. Capt. Felix H. Robertson was ordered to report to me with his own and Capt. H. C. Semple's batteries of Napoleon guns. Captain Wright, who with his battery had been detached some days before, was ordered to join his brigade (Preston's). The brigades of Adams and Preston, which were left on the west side of the river Wednesday night, had been ordered to rejoin me. At the moment of my advance our artillery in the center and on the left was to open on the enemy. One gun from our center was the signal for the attack. The commanding general desired that the attack should be made with the least possible delay.

"It was now 2:30 p. m. Two of the brigades had to march two miles and the other one mile. Brigadier-General Pillow, having reported for duty, was assigned by the commanding general to Col. Joseph B. Palmer's brigade, and that fine officer resumed command of his regiment and was three times wounded during the ensuing engagement. The Ninth Kentucky and Cobb's battery, under the command of Colonel Hunt, were left to hold the hill so often referred to.

"The division, after deducting the losses of Wednesday, the troops left on the hill and companies in special service, consisted of some 4,500 men. It was drawn up in two lines, the first in a narrow skirt of woods, the second two hundred yards in rear. Pillow and Hanson formed the first line, Pillow on the right. Preston supported Pillow, and Adams' brigade (commanded by Col. R. L. Gibson) supported Hanson. The artillery was placed in rear of the second line, under orders to move with it and occupy the summit of the slope as soon as the infantry should rout the enemy. Feeling anxious about my right, I sent two staff officers in succession to communicate with Pegram and Wharton, but received no intelligence up to the moment of assault. The interval between my left and the troops on the hill was already too great, but I had a battery to watch it and a small infantry support. There was nothing to prevent the enemy from observing nearly all our movements and preparations. To reach him it was necessary to cross an open space 600 or 700 yards in width, with a gentle ascent,

"I had informed the commanding general that we would be ready to advance at 4 o'clock, and precisely at that hour the signal gun was heard from our center. Instantly the troops moved forward at a quickstep and in admirable order. The front line had bayonets fixed, with orders to deliver one volley and then use the bayonet.

"The fire of the enemy's artillery on both sides the river commenced as soon as the troops entered the open ground. When less than half the distance across the field, the quick eye of O'Hara discovered a force extending considerably beyond our right. I immediately directed Major Graves to move a battery to our right and open on them. He at once advanced Wright's battery and effectually checked their movements. Before our line reached the enemy's position, his artillery fire became heavy, accurate and destructive. Many officers and men fell before we closed with their infantry, yet our brave fellows pushed forward with the utmost determination and after a brief but bloody conflict routed both opposing lines, took four hundred prisoners and several flags, and drove their artillery and the great body of their infantry across the river. Many were killed at the water's edge. Their artillery took time by the forelock in crossing the stream. A few of our men in their ardor actually crossed over before they could be prevented, most of whom subsequently moving up the west bank recrossed at a ford three-quarters of a mile above. The second line had halted when the first engaged the enemy's infantry, and laid down under orders; but very soon the casualties in the first line, the fact that the artillery on the opposite line was more fatal to the second line than the first, and the eagerness of the troops, impelled them forward, and at the decisive moment when the opposing infantry was routed, the two lines had mingled into one, the only practical inconvenience of which was that at several points the ranks were deeper than is allowed by proper military formation.

"A strong force of the enemy beyond our extreme right yet remained on the east side of the river. Presently a new line of battle appeared on the west bank, directly opposite our troops, and opened fire, while at the same time large masses crossed in front of our right and advanced to the attack. We were compelled to fall back. As soon as our infantry had won the ridge, Major Graves advanced the artillery of the division and opened fire. At the same time Captain Robertson threw forward Semple's battery toward our right, which did excellent service. He did not advance his own battery (which was to have taken position on the left), supposing that that part of the field had not been cleared of the enemy's infantry. Although mistaken in this, since the enemy had been driven across the river, yet I regard it as fortunate that the battery was not brought forward. It would have been a vain contest.

"It now appeared that the ground we had won was commanded by the enemy's batteries within easy range on better ground on the other side of the river. I know not how many guns he had.* He had enough to sweep the whole position from the front, the left and the right, and to render it wholly untenable by our force present of artillery and infantry. The infantry, after passing the crest and descending the slope toward the river, were in some measure protected, and suffered less at this period of the action than the artillery.

"We lost three guns, nearly all the horses being killed, and not having the time or men to draw them off by hand.

"One was lost because there was but one boy left (Private Wright, of Wright's battery) to limber the piece, and his strength was unequal to it.

"The command fell back in some disorder, but without the slightest appearance of panic, and reformed behind Robertson's battery in the narrow skirt of timber from which we emerged to the assault. The enemy did not advance beyond the position in which he received our attack. My skirmishers continued to occupy a part of the field over which we had advanced until the army retired from Murfreesboro. The action lasted about one hour and twenty minutes. As our lines advanced to the attack several rounds of artillery were heard from our center, apparently directed against the enemy on the west bank of the river.

"At twilight Brig.-Gen. Patton Anderson reported to me with his brigade, and remained in position with me until the army retired. I took up line of battle for the night a little in rear of the field over which we advanced to the assault, and Captain Robertson at my request disposed the artillery in the positions indicated for it. Many of the reports do not discriminate between the losses of Wednesday and Friday. The total loss of my division, exclusive of Jackson's command, is 2,140, of which I think 1,700 occurred on Friday. The loss of the enemy on this day was, I think, greater than our own, since he suffered immense slaughter between the ridge and the river.

"I cannot forbear to express my admiration for the courage and constancy of the troops, exhibited even after it became apparent that the main object could not be accomplished. Beyond the general good conduct, a number of enlisted men displayed at different times of the action the most heroic bravery. I respectfully suggest that authority be given to select a certain number of the most distinguished in each brigade to be recommended to the President for promotion.

*It is said there were fifty-five guns.

"I cannot enumerate all the brave officers who fell, nor the living who did their duty; yet I may be permitted to lament, in common with the army, the premature death of Brigadier-General Hanson, who received a mortal wound at the moment the enemy began to give way. Endeared to his friends by his private virtues, and to his command by the vigilance with which he guarded its interest and honor, he was by the universal testimony of his military associates one of the finest officers that adorned the service of the Confederate States. Upon his fall the command devolved upon Colonel Trabue, who in another organization had long and ably commanded most of the regiments composing the brigade.

"I cannot close without expressing my obligations to the gentlemen of my staff. This is no formal acknowledgment. I can never forget that during all the operations they were ever prompt and cheerful, by night and day, in conveying orders, conducting to their positions regiments and brigades, rallying troops in the field, and, indeed, in the discharge of every duty. It gives me pleasure to name Lieutenant-Colonel Buckner, assistant adjutant-general, who was absent on leave, but returned upon the first rumor of battle; Colonel O'Hara, acting adjutant-general, Lieutenant Breckinridge, aide-de-camp; Major Graves, chief of artillery (twice wounded and his horse shot under him); Maj. James Wilson, assistant inspector-general (horse shot); Capt. Charles Semple, ordnance officer; Lieutenant Darragh, severely wounded. Captains Martin and Coleman, of my volunteer staff, were active and efficient. The former had his horse killed under him.

"Drs. J. F. Heustis and J. E. Pendleton, chief surgeon and medical inspector, were unremitting in their attention to the wounded. Dr. Stanhope Breckinridge, assistant surgeon, accompanied my headquarters and pursued his duties through the fire of Wednesday. Mr. Buckner, and Mr. Zantzinger, of Kentucky, attached themselves to me for the occasion and were active. Capt. E. M. Blackburn, commanding my escort, ever cool and vigilant, rendered essential service and made several bold reconnoissances. Charles Chotard, of the escort, acting as my orderly on Wednesday, displayed much gallantry and intelligence.

"The army retired before daybreak on the morning of the 4th. My division, moving on the Manchester road, was the rear of Hardee's corps. The Ninth Kentucky, Forty-first Alabama, and

Cobb's battery, all under the command of Colonel Hunt, formed a special rear guard. The enemy did not follow us.

"My acknowledgments are due to Col. J. Stoddard Johnston, Lieutenant-Colonel Brent, and Lieutenant-Colonel Garner, of General Bragg's staff, and to Major Pickett of Lieutenant-General Hardee's staff, for services on Friday, January 2nd."

Many a home in Kentucky was filled with mourning by this battle, and the Orphan brigade long lamented the death of its beloved commander. Gen. Roger Weightman Hanson had served as lieutenant in the Mexican war, and to great gallantry as a soldier and the accomplishments of an able lawyer united the rare qualities which made him respected as a commander and endeared to all as a comrade. As colonel of the Second Kentucky, whose fate he shared at Donelson, he had brought it up to the highest standard of discipline, and had already, in the brief interval since his promotion, given to his brigade a reputation of the first prominence. He was struck in the left thigh with the leaden strap of a rifle shell, causing a wound, which, though serious, was not regarded as mortal. As he was being borne in an ambulance to Murfreesboro, he passed near the center where were General Polk and other officers who expressed their sympathy. He was cheerful and to the hope expressed by the bishop-general that he would soon recover, replied that it was a serious wound, but added that it was glorious to die for one's country. His devoted wife received his shattered form, but the shock to his system was too great for the skill of the surgeon, and he died on the morning of the 4th. Another wife, Mrs. Breckinridge, had shared the anxiety of this Spartan woman, and with heroic fortitude cheered her with her sympathy. She had for two days listened to the thunder of artillery, while her husband and two sons were exposed to its fire, and was not only sustained through this ordeal and in her ministrations to her less fortunate friend, but, when the army retreated, she left at midnight in an ambulance, having in charge Maj. Rice E. Graves, chief of artillery on General Breckinridge's staff, who had been severely wounded, bore him safely to Chattanooga, a distance of nearly a hundred miles over the mountains, and then nursed him until he was able to return to duty. Such were the trials which the women of the South had to meet, and they did it with the same heroism shown by their husbands, sons and brothers in the field.

Saturday which followed the battle was a cold, drizzly day,

marked by no military operations on either side. The Confederate troops, having been for a week in the front line of battle, crippled by its casualties and outnumbered by the enemy, were evidently unfit for further aggression or resistance. It was accordingly decided by a council of war to fall back, and at nightfall the retreat began in the order named in General Bragg's memoranda before the battle of the first day, General Polk's corps moving to Shelbyville and General Hardee's to Manchester. The movement was in perfect order and apparently without the knowledge of the enemy, from whom there was no molestation. General Bragg established his headquarters at Tullahoma, and the army remained in that vicinity, not more than forty miles from Murfreesboro, and in possession of the country to within ten or twelve miles of it, for more than five months.

About ten days before the battle of Murfreesboro Gen. John H. Morgan started on one of his celebrated raids against Rosecrans' communications in Kentucky, which, had General Bragg on a decisive battle, would have been very disastrous in its results. He moved by his well-beaten path to Glasgow, Ky., encountering opposition there and at Cave City, but crossing Green river did great damage along the railroad from Bacon Creek bridge to Elizabethtown, where he captured six hundred prisoners, and made a circuit by way of Springfield and Columbia to Burkesville, where he crossed the Cumberland on the 2nd. Notwithstanding the severe weather, hard marching and fighting, his loss was but two killed, twenty-four wounded and sixty-four missing, while he captured 1,877 prisoners, with a large amount of stores and arms, and diverted the attention of a large force of the enemy, whose cavalry showed great improvement in efficiency. His absence was keenly felt by General Bragg, who during the critical week at Murfreesboro sought to bring him to his aid, but he was too remote for communication in time. The Confederate Congress, in recognition of the service, tendered thanks to "Gen. John H. Morgan and his men for their varied, heroic and invaluable services in Tennessee and Kentucky on this expedition—services which have conferred upon them fame as enduring as the records of the struggle which they have so brilliantly illustrated." Shortly after his return General Bragg recommended his promotion to a major-general.

CHAPTER XVI

GENERAL BRAGG'S ARMY IN WINTER QUARTERS — DEATH OF COLONEL TRABUE — VISIT OF GENERAL JOSEPH E. JOHNSTON — DRILLS AND REVIEWS — THEODORE O'HARA — CONFEDERATE REVERSES — GENERAL BRECKINRIDGE'S DIVISION SENT TO MISSISSIPPI — GENERAL BUCKNER ASSIGNED TO THE COMMAND OF THE DEPARTMENT OF EAST TENNESSEE, AND GENERAL PRESTON TO THAT OF SOUTHWEST VIRGINIA — FALL OF VICKSBURG — OPERATIONS IN MISSISSIPPI — CAPTURE OF COLONEL STREIGHT'S COMMAND BY GENERAL FORREST — FEDERAL ADVANCE IN TENNESSEE — MORGAN'S GREAT RAID THROUGH OHIO

GENERAL BRAGG'S army was in comfortable condition during the winter, the main work being done by the cavalry, which was kept well to the front to give as extensive foraging ground as possible, General Morgan's command being about McMinnville and having occasional skirmishes and small battles with detachments of the enemy. Col. R. P. Trabue succeeded General Hanson in command of the Orphan brigade until the arrival of Brig.-Gen. Ben Hardin Helm, who had recovered from the injury to his leg, broken by the fall of his horse at Baton Rouge. Colonel Trabue, to the sorrow of his regiment and the brigade, died in Richmond, Va., February 12, 1863. The army was kept in a good state of discipline by frequent reviews and drilling, in which the Kentucky brigade, by general consent, bore off the palm. On the 19th of March Gen. J. E. Johnston came to Tullahoma and being the senior officer, it was expected that he would as such supersede General Bragg; but although he remained nearly two months, he declined to take active command, but co-operated with Bragg in all matters concerning the army, at the same time retaining command of department No. 2, which also included Mississippi. In honor of his arrival there was a grand review in which General Hardee introduced the charge of a brigade in line of battle, by regiments, with a shout, at double-quick time. It was then that General Johnston paid the Orphan brigade the compliment of saying that they were the equal of any regular troops he had ever seen. It was a gala day for the Kentuckians. A flag which had been made by Mrs. Breckinridge was presented to the 20th Tennessee, of General Preston's brigade, in her behalf, by Col. Theodore O'Hara, of General Breckinridge's staff, author of the "Bivouac of the Dead," who proved himself an orator as well as a poet.

As spring advanced, Hardee's corps was moved up nearer to the front, Breckinridge being placed at Beech Grove, 12 miles from Murfreesboro, and in special charge of Hoover's Gap, an important point in General Bragg's line through which Rosecrans, during the summer, advanced. The month of May was marked by great activity in the armies, both of the East and West. The victories of Chancellorsville and Fredericksburg, marred by the death of Stonewall Jackson, occurred on the 2nd and 4th. On the 14th the Federal army, having got into the rear of Vicksburg, captured Jackson, Miss. On the 10th Gen. Joseph E. Johnston had left Tullahoma with two brigades to reinforce the Confederate army at Jackson and to take command, but was too late to save the position, and applied for reinforcements. On the 24th, General Breckinridge with his division was ordered to that point. Colonel Hunt of the Fifth, whose family had been sent through the lines from Kentucky, was compelled to resign, and was succeeded by Lieut.-Col. J. W. Caldwell. General Preston was in May ordered to the command of the department of Southwestern Virginia, to succeed Gen. Humphrey Marshall, and about the same time General Buckner was transferred from Mobile to command the department of East Tennessee. With the departure of General Breckinridge on the 25th there were no Kentucky troops left in Tennessee except the cavalry.

Upon the arrival of his division in Mississippi, June 1st, the enemy had evacuated Jackson, and General Breckinridge was placed in command at that place. His division was now composed of Adams', Evans', Stovall's and Helm's brigades, the Forty-seventh Georgia, and Waters' South Carolina battery, reporting 8,194 for duty. There were also in Johnston's army the majority of the Kentucky troops, the Third, Seventh and Eighth regiments, with many Kentucky officers assigned to important duties. Gen. Lloyd Tilghman, a most gallant officer, had been killed in the Baker's Creek battle, near Edwards' Depot, a short time before; Gen. Abram Buford and Gen. Geo. B. Cosby were in command of cavalry brigades, and Dr. D. W. Yandell had become medical director on General Johnston's staff.

The campaign which followed was one of great hardship and of small results; the weary marches, the un-healthful climate and bad drinking water being especially severe on the Kentuckians. Vicksburg fell on the 4th of July, and with the battle of Gettysburg just preceding, marked a fatal turning point in the fortunes of the Confederacy. The only engagement of any note in which General Breckinridge's command participated was on the 12th of July, near Jackson, in which he repulsed the enemy. But General Grant's army being free to move from Vicksburg, General Johnston retired from Jackson and took a position fifty miles eastward where he was free from further molestation. Here General Breckinridge's division remained until August 26th, when it was ordered to Chattanooga, which had now become the storm center in the West.

General Rosecrans, pending the military operations in the southwest, and his own preparations for a general advance, had long remained quiescent. About the 20th of June he gave evidence of a positive advance, both with his own army and one commanded by General Burnside, into East Tennessee. An extensive cavalry raid was made here by Colonel Carter, who approached the vicinity of Knoxville, and burned several bridges on the East Tennessee & Virginia railroad. On the 23rd of June General Rosecrans captured Hoover's Gap and General Bragg fell back gradually to Chattanooga, when the situation became very similar to that of a year previous, when General Buell on the right and Gen. Geo. W. Morgan on the left seemed on the point of success. But the waste of a year upon the vital force of the South from losses in battle, and the exhaustion of her resources from the blockading of her ports, together with the vast army of the North, recruited from every nation, and with unlimited supplies, domestic and imported, were telling severely upon the Southern cause. In the retrospect it is not strange that defeat ensued, but that it was postponed nearly two years.

The only success scored by General Bragg's forces since the battle of Murfreesboro had been the brilliant capture during the winter of Streight's brigade of cavalry by General Forrest. The Federal raid had been made through the mountains of North Alabama with a view of the capture of Rome, Ga., and the destruction of the Confederate arsenal there. Forrest pursued and after an extraordinary and prolonged march on the trail of his adversary, captured the entire command, when within fifteen or twenty miles of their destination. The boldness of the Federal enterprise was only excelled by the brilliancy of the Confederate success.

But now, when the Federal infantry was advancing, General Morgan executed a movement for the diversion of the enemy, which in its conception and details constituted the most remarkable cavalry exploit of the war. Moving to the rear of Rosecrans with his cavalry division of 2,300 men, he crossed the Cumberland river at Burkesville on the 2d of July, passed through Columbia, Lebanon and Bardstown to Brandenburg, forty miles below Louisville, and there on the 8th crossed the Ohio into Indiana, drawing after him large bodies of Federal cavalry and infantry and having a number of heavy engagements. Thence he swept through Corydon, Salem and other towns, until on the 13th he was in the vicinity of Cincinnati, having captured many troops, and with the hue and cry of two States raised against him. He was pursued and sought to be headed by large bodies of the enemy's cavalry and infantry, drawn from all quarters. With little time for rest he directed his course northeastward through Ohio until, worn down by fatigue and encompassed by overwhelming odds in his rear, on his flank, and in front, including troops in steamers moving by the Ohio, a large part of his force while attempting to cross into West Virginia at Buffington's Island was captured on the 21st of July, and on the 26th General Morgan was forced to surrender with as many more, bringing the aggregate of his loss to more than half of his original command. The remainder made their way to the South in small detachments and were organized at Abingdon, Va. Of the imprisonment of General Morgan and his principal officers in the penitentiary at Columbus, Ohio, his romantic escape from therewith six of his faithful comrades, Hines, Hochersmith, Sheldon, Bennett, McGee and Taylor, and of his subsequent movements and tragic death, September 4, 1864, at Greeneville, Tenn., reference must be made to the full and able history of Morgan's cavalry by his distinguished second in command, Gen. Basil W. Duke. The proper record of the bold enterprises and dashing exploits of this great cavalry leader would of themselves alone require more space than is accorded to this general narrative of the part taken in the war by all the Kentuckians who followed the Confederate banner.

CHAPTER XVII

ROSECRANS FLANKS CHATTANOOGA AND BRAGG EVACUATES – BURNSIDE ENTERS EAST TENNESSEE AND BUCKNER JOINS BRAGG – MOVEMENTS OF OPPOSING ARMIES PRECEDING BATTLE – LONGSTREET JOINS BRAGG WITH HIS CORPS – BATTLE OF CHICKAMAUGA – ARRANGEMENT OF LINES OF BATTLE – IMPORTANT PART PLAYED BY KENTUCKY OFFICERS AND SOLDIERS – SEVERE LOSSES – DEATH OF GENERAL BEN HARDIN HELM AND COLONEL JAMES HEWITT – GREAT CONFEDERATE VICTORY – CHARLES A. DANA'S OPINION – BRECKINRIDGE, BUCKNER AND PRESTON

THE danger threatening Chattanooga and east Tennessee now called for the concentration of all the troops which could be made available for its defenses. Rosecrans advanced slowly and cautiously, while Bragg was busily engaged in fortifying at Chattanooga, through the months of July and August. Rosecrans, declining a direct attack, projected a heavy movement up Will's valley on the western side of Lookout mountain, threatening Rome and Bragg's communications, thus forcing the evacuation of Chattanooga on the 9th day of September, Bragg's object being by a coup to crush the right wing of Rosecrans' army, which was moving into Georgia through the gaps south of Chattanooga, and then to turn suddenly upon its left, which occupied the city.

Meanwhile, General Burnside having advanced into east Tennessee from Kentucky, General Buckner had evacuated Knoxville on the 25th of August, and joined Bragg with his division, commanded by General Preston, who with the Fifth Kentucky and some other troops came from southwest Virginia to reinforce General Bragg. Buckner was then placed in command of a corps consisting of the divisions of Gen. A. P. Stewart and General Preston, the latter embracing the troops of General Buckner's department, composed of Gracie's, Trigg's and Kelly's brigades. General Breckinridge's division, which had previously arrived from Mississippi, was placed in the corps of Gen. D. H. Hill.

When General Bragg moved out of Chattanooga to attack Rosecrans' flanking corps, his Federal opponent thought he was in full retreat toward Rome. Crittenden's corps was therefore started after him and proceeded as far as Ringgold, when it was discovered that the report was false. Bragg's whole army was between the wings of Rosecrans', which were almost fifty miles apart. He tried to crush the right wing under Thomas at McLemore's Cove, but it evaded battle and with McCook's and Crittenden's corps turned toward Chattanooga for better security. Bragg then also moved towards Chattanooga, aiming to intercept Rosecrans and cut him off from his stronghold. On the afternoon of the 18th of September he crossed Chickamauga creek at Lee & Gordon's mill, with the view of throwing himself across the main road leading from Crawfish Springs to Chattanooga. Thomas, divining his purpose, crossed the creek at Crawfish Springs and by a night march parallel to Bragg, secured the position he occupied in the subsequent battle.

The morning of the 19th found Bragg in the act of forming his line in a direction generally parallel with the road to Chattanooga, with his left wing resting on the Chickamauga at Lee & Gordon's mill. General Buckner's corps was placed on the left, with Preston's division at Lee & Gordon's mill, and Stewart's on his right. General Longstreet, whose corps had arrived from Virginia the day before, was on Buckner's right. Hill's corps and Polk's corps were still on the east side of the Chickamauga. While General Bragg was making his alignment on the morning of the 19th his right came in contact with part of the Federal forces under General Thomas, and a heavy engagement ensued in the thick woods, which prevented either side from determining well what was in its front. In the afternoon, General Preston's division was for a time hotly engaged, but repulsed the attack and held its position with the loss of 150 men killed and wounded. The enemy had also suffered on our right, but the army not being united, further advance was not made.

At night both armies prepared for the great battle of the next day. General Breckinridge crossed the river and at daylight was placed on the extreme right, his left resting on the right of Cleburne's division. General Polk was in command of the right wing, consisting of his own and Hill's corps; and General Longstreet of the left, composed of his own and Buckner's corps. During the night, General Thomas, who had been severely pressed the day before, had felled timber and made a breastwork in the thick forest of small trees parallel to our line, so located as not to be discernible until closely approached. These works covered Breckinridge's left and Cleburne's right. The break of day found the two armies in lines of nearly equal length, the

Federals near and a little in front of the main Chattanooga road, McCook's corps on the right, his right resting on Crawfish Springs, Crittenden's in center, and Thomas' on the left, and the Confederates a few hundred yards east of them.

It had been Bragg's intention to attack early in the morning, but there was delay in perfecting his dispositions on the right in support of Cleburne, and to his left, and it was not until half-past nine that the advance was made. The thick woods and generally level nature of the ground prevented the use of much artillery, and until positions were changed later in the day, but little was used.

Bragg's plan of battle was that which characterized his other fights, to open on the right and swing on his left as a pivot. Rosecrans' policy was, as at Murfreesboro, waiting and defensive. Breckinridge's division was posted as follows: Helm's Kentucky brigade on the left, Stovall's in the center, and Adams' on the right. At the hour named the advance was made and in a few minutes the battle opened with great fury, extending to the right of Longstreet's line; but that part of the line which came upon the breastworks of Thomas met with heavy loss and was forced to fall back after having advanced within pistol shot of it.

General Breckinridge in his report says: "The battle was opened by Helm with great fury. The Second and Ninth Kentucky, with three companies of the Forty-first Alabama regiment, encountered the left of a line of breastworks before reaching the Chattanooga road, and though assailing them with great courage, were compelled to pause. From some cause the line on my left had not advanced simultaneously with my division, and in consequence these brave troops were at first, in addition to the fire in front, subjected to a severe enfilading fire from the left. The rest of Helm's brigade, in whose front there were no works, after a short but sharp engagement, routed a line of the enemy, pursued it across the Chattanooga road, and captured a section of artillery in the center of the road. This portion of the brigade was now brought under a heavy and enfilading fire, and being separated from its left, I ordered Col. Jos. H. Lewis of the Sixth Kentucky, who succeeded to the command upon the fall of General Helm, to withdraw the troops some two hundred yards to the rear, reunite the brigade and change his front slightly to meet the new order of things by throwing forward his right and retiring his left. The movement was made without panic or confusion.

"This was one of the bloodiest encounters of the day. Here General Helm, ever ready for action, and endeared to his command by his many virtues, received a mortal wound, while in the heroic discharge of duty. Col. J. W. Hewitt of the Second Kentucky was killed, acting gallantly at the head of his regiment. Captains Madeira, Rogers, and Dedman, of the Second, Captain Daniel of the Ninth Kentucky, and many officers and men met their deaths before the enemy's works; while Colonel Nuckols of the Fourth Kentucky, Colonel Caldwell of the Ninth, and many more officers and men, were wounded.

"In the meantime Adams and Stovall advanced steadily, driving two lines of skirmishers. Stovall halted at the Chattanooga road. Adams, after dispersing a regiment and capturing a battery, crossed at Glenn's farm and halted a short distance beyond in an open field. When Helm's brigade was checked, and I had given Colonel Lewis orders in reference to his new position, I rode to the commands of Adams and Stovall on the right. It was now evident from the comparatively slight resistance they had encountered and the fact they were not threatened in front, that our line extended beyond the enemy's left. I at once ordered these brigades to change front perpendicularly to the original line of battle, and with the left of Adams and the right of Stovall resting on the Chattanooga road, to advance upon the flank of the enemy. Slocomb's battery, which had previously done good service, was posted on favorable ground on the west of the road to support the movement. The brigades moved in fine order over a field and entered the woods beyond. Stovall soon encountered the extreme left of the enemy's works, which retiring from the general north and south direction of his intrenchments, extended westward to the Chattanooga road. After a severe and well-contested conflict, he was checked and forced to retire. Adams on the west side of the road met two lines of the enemy, who had improved the short time to bring up reinforcements and reform nearly at right angles to the troops in his main line of works." General Breckinridge compliments Cobb's battery for its action in the fight.

Some further fighting occurred here, but General Breckinridge, finding himself confronted by a largely superior force and having no support, after getting actually in rear of Thomas' main line, reformed his command east of the Chattanooga road, about six hundred yards in front of his first line of the morning. His account of this movement, in advancing independently, and upon his own responsibility changing front, and moving upon the enemy's flank and rear, has been presented here for the purpose of giving him the credit which his modesty prevented him from claiming and his superiors failed to recognize as it deserved. Its bearing upon the result of the battle and its immediate effect upon the enemy were such that it led directly to the disaster which soon befell the Federal army. When the Confederate line had recoiled from Thomas' breastworks, the assault was renewed by fresh lines, and this, together with the threatened danger to Thomas' rear by Breckinridge's movement, led to the transfer of heavy reinforcements from the Federal right and center, leaving a gap in front of General Hood, who threw his division forward promptly and broke their line, inflicting heavy loss upon the enemy and being himself desperately wounded. The movement was taken up in line by Stewart's division of Buckner's corps and later by Preston's division, which drove all before them with great slaughter, until it became in the nature of a right wheel on the left center; and the greater part of the left wing advanced across the Chattanooga road, assuming a line almost at right angles to its former position.

Thus with his right broken up and bent back, and with renewed charges upon Thomas' breastworks and a fresh advance of Breckinridge, the entire Federal right was beaten back toward the foothills of Missionary Ridge in the rear. Lately published reminiscences of Charles A. Dana, assistant secretary of war, who was on the field, fully confirm this view. He says Rosecrans' defeat was a veritable Bull Run. There remained but one point of Federal resistance besides that of Thomas, and this was the wooded hills near McFarland's Gap and the key to the Federal position.

General Preston, who had as a guide Dyer, whose house stood on the battlefield near by, and from whom he learned the nature of the topography in the front, followed after Hindman's and McLaws' divisions, which had met a heavy repulse, and moving up a ravine beyond Snodgrass' house, charged the flank of Granger and Steedman, posted with artillery on commanding ridges. It was bloody but effective work, resulting in the complete rout of the enemy and the capture of the Eighty-ninth Ohio, the Twenty-second Michigan, and part of the Twenty-first Ohio regiments. This bold and decisive stroke, which closed the battle as the sun set, was one of the most gallant affairs of the war, and like that of Breckinridge on the right was made upon General Preston's own judgment, as he was ordered originally merely to support Hindman. A British officer present compared Preston to Dessaix and said his charge was one of the greatest in history. The Fifth Kentucky, Colonel Hawkins, was conspicuous for gallantry in this fight.

In the confusion resulting from the change of lines, the smoke of battle, and approach of night, it was difficult to comprehend the full extent of this Confederate victory. The enemy, beaten at every point, availing himself of the favorable conditions, retreated in the direction of Chattanooga, and the Confederate army, worn down by long and arduous labors, with all commands mingled in promiscuous confusion, went to sleep on the battlefield, each where he found himself. The further details of what followed, the fatality which, arising partly from the want of sufficient force, but chiefly from the lack of Stonewall Jackson persistence, lost the full fruits of victory, belong to general history. It has been the aim in this narrative to sketch briefly only so much of the battle as will show to their countrymen the part performed by the Confederate soldiers from Kentucky and their gallant officers. For small, yet effective, as were the number of muskets, no troops fought more bravely, and no State was more ably represented than Kentucky in her trio of generals, —noble men all, who were never separated in friendship by faction or jealousy, and who illustrated in their character and deeds the elements which make men great and have made their State famous. Each, by the unanimous verdict of the army, earned an advancement in grade; but Kentucky was already top-heavy in rank proportionate to her troops in the service, and other States clamored for recognition of their sons. Later in the war General Buckner was made a lieutenant-general, and just before its close General Preston a major-general.

CHAPTER XVIII

INVESTMENT OF CHATTANOOGA BY BRAGG — GENERAL ROSECRANS DISPLACED BY GENERAL GRANT — BATTLE OF MISSIONARY RIDGE — GENERAL BUCKNER ASSIGNED TO THE TRANS-MISSISSIPPI DEPARTMENT — GENERAL PRESTON APPOINTED MINISTER TO MEXICO AND GENERAL BRECKINRIDGE ASSIGNED TO THE DEPARTMENT OF SOUTHWEST VIRGINIA — SAD PARTING OF THE LATTER WITH THE KENTUCKY BRIGADE — GENERAL JOSEPH E. JOHNSTON SUCCEEDS BRAGG — HIS COMPLIMENT TO THE BRIGADE — BRECKINRIDGE'S SERVICE IN VIRGINIA — HIS VICTORY OVER SIGEL AT NEW MARKET — HIS OVATION FROM GENERAL LEE'S ARMY — BATTLE OF SECOND COLD HARBOR — MONOCACY — IN SIGHT OF WASHINGTON CITY — SHENANDOAH VALLEY CAMPAIGN — RETURN TO HIS DEPARTMENT — KENTUCKY TROOPS THERE AND OPERATIONS — MADE SECRETARY OF WAR — SUCCEEDING EVENTS

THE second day after the battle, General Bragg moved up to within cannon-shot of Chattanooga, where Rosecrans, reassured by the failure of pursuit and the strength of the defenses which Bragg had constructed, suspended his movements for retreat inaugurated in the Federal panic, and settled down to stand a siege. Bragg disposed his army in the valley between Missionary Ridge and Point Lookout, from which latter elevation every movement in the beleaguered town was distinctly visible. He remained there until November 25th. Meanwhile Burnside had captured Knoxville, and Longstreet was sent to dislodge him, but was foiled, after a desperate assault on the strong fortifications, and the greater part of East Tennessee was permanently lost to the Confederacy. At the same time Federal reinforcements poured into Chattanooga, and General Grant, full of the prestige of Vicksburg and looming up into the prominence which soon placed him at the head of the Federal armies, was sent to restore the shattered confidence of Rosecrans' army. The result is told in few words.

The "Battle of the Clouds" on Lookout Mountain is a myth. The battle of Missionary Ridge was little short of a disgrace. The resistance was as feeble as that of many of the detachments which Morgan captured in his raids, and with the loss of a few hundred the Confederate army fell back beyond the Chickamauga and went into winter quarters at Dalton, Ga. With it went the Kentucky brigade, farther and farther from home, yet with the same brave and loyal spirit which ever characterized it.

General Preston had, before the battle of Missionary Ridge, been restored to his department in southwestern Virginia, but had left the Fifth Kentucky, which became permanently a part of the Orphan brigade. In a short time he was sent as minister to Mexico, and his military career ceased. In his place General Buckner was ordered to Virginia, and after a brief service was, at his own request, assigned to the Trans-Mississippi, and was thenceforward separated from the Kentucky troops with whom he had so long been associated. In common with many other officers from Kentucky and elsewhere, he had been involved in unpleasant controversy with General Bragg, and longer service in his department became distasteful. Thus almost simultaneously the army of Tennessee, as it was still called, lost two of its most conspicuous officers. But it was soon to lose a third. President Davis, recognizing the capacity and influence of General Breckinridge, and the demand for an officer of his merit in that field, in the early part of February tendered him the command of the department of Southwestern Virginia, and he accepted it. The announcement of the fact brought gloom to the Kentucky brigade, and the parting was touching. The night before he left they called in a body to take leave of him, and besought him to secure their transfer to his department. When he went to Richmond on his way to take command, he made the application, and afterward repeated it urgently; but when the matter was referred to Gen. Joseph E. Johnston, who had succeeded General Bragg in the command, that officer disapproved the transfer, saying in compliment to the brigade, which ever endeared him to it, that its place could not be supplied. Thus the year 1864 started off with a general shake-up in the army at Dalton, and the several officers went to their new fields of service, not again to be united.

Leaving the Kentucky brigade in quarters at Dalton for a season of rest and recreation, a brief record will be made of General Breckinridge's after service and that of the Kentuckians who came under his command, as little account has ever been made of it within the reach of his admiring countrymen.

The department to which he had been assigned was one of great territorial dimensions, and of an altogether inadequate force. It extended from the Alleghany mountains as far west in East Tennessee as was held by the Confederate arms, and northward the same. It had been the graveyard of Confederate generals as far as their reputations were concerned, owing to the fact that, with a front of nearly three hundred miles open to invasions of the enemy by routes impossible to guard, whenever it was invaded blame fell upon the commanding general and his prestige was destroyed. It came near being the ruin of General Lee, while Floyd, Loring and a number of others were in turn retired and their future usefulness destroyed.

In the latter part of February General Breckinridge assumed command of the department with headquarters at Dublin Depot, Pulaski county, on the East Tennessee and Virginia railroad, a few miles west of New River. One of his first acts was to make a horseback tour along his front, extending from Warm Springs on the northeast to Abingdon, involving a ride of three hundred miles in wintry weather. His infantry consisted of two brigades, that of Gen. John Echols, at Monroe Draught, near the Greenbrier White Sulphur Springs, and that of Gen. G. C. Wharton, at the Narrows of New River. At Warm Springs was a cavalry brigade under Gen. W. L. Jackson, and other detachments of cavalry were at other widely separate stations, of which there were sixteen and with which communication was chiefly by courier. Gen. John H. Morgan, who had reorganized the remnant of his command, was in the vicinity of Abingdon, and there also were the brigades of Gen. H. L. Giltner and Geo. B. Cosby, chiefly composed of Kentuckians, while other bodies of cavalry not necessary to enumerate, detached and of smaller numbers, were disposed with reference to scouting, forage and subsistence. Within his department were the Wythe county lead mines, from which came the principal supply for the armies of the Confederacy, and the salt works at Saltville, from which was derived in great part the salt necessary for the whole South, east of the Mississippi. Added to these features was the fact that soon after he took command General Longstreet, who had occupied that part of East Tennessee not held by the Federal forces, was called to

Northern Virginia, increasing largely the responsibility of his charge. His coming was greeted warmly by the people of that part of Virginia, and by the troops to whom his high reputation was an assurance of an improved service. He had, however, not long been in command when the campaign in Eastern Virginia began, and on the 5th day of May, when he was preparing to resist an invasion from the Kanawha valley, he received a dispatch from General Lee, who was engaged in the battles of the Wilderness, to move at once with all his available force to Staunton for the defense of that point, and defend it against Sigel, who was moving up the Shenandoah valley. Breckinridge started immediately with his two infantry brigades for a long march over the mountains, and arrived at Staunton on the 11th, calling out the militia of Augusta county and the cadets of the Virginia military institute at Lexington. It was generally supposed that he would fortify and await Sigel's advance, but on the 13th he put his forces, numbering about 3,500, including a small cavalry force under General Imboden, in motion to meet Sigel, who was reported about fifty miles northward.

On the evening of the 14th he had reached a point within nine miles of New Market, near which and to the north he learned that Sigel was camped. At one o'clock that night, the weather being rainy, he marched north, and at daylight on the morning of Sunday, May 15th, his infantry was in line of battle just south of New Market, almost within cannon shot of Sigel before that officer knew there was any infantry force between him and Staunton. There was little delay for preliminaries, and by noon Sigel, who had about twice the number of troops led by Breckinridge, had been forced to fall back beyond New Market, where he took a strong position on the crest of a hill from which there was a gentle slope of nearly a mile through wheat-fields and blue-grass pastures. General Breckinridge was reluctant to put the cadets, of whom there were 225, into the battle and at first proposed to detach them as rear guard to the trains, but they pleaded so earnestly that he finally yielded and gave them the post of honor in the center, between the two brigades, as a color line for them to dress by. He had but one line, but his flanks were protected by a bluff bank of the Shenandoah on the left, and swampy ground at the right. From the nature of the topography, he could not use artillery directly, but ascertaining by reconnoitering that he could move it to an eligible position on the right and advance even with, or a little in front of his line, he moved his command up, while with the artillery, whose fire he directed, he selected for his own post the right, where he kept himself in view of his troops and inspired them by his presence. The line moved in spirited order in the face of a galling fire; while advancing his artillery, consisting of ten pieces, he secured somewhat of an enfilading or quartering fire upon the enemy and diverted their attention in the interest of the infantry. Its effect was felt first by Sigel's reserve line, among which arose confusion, which Sigel sought to counteract by a cavalry charge from the left of his line; but canister soon repulsed that, and in a short time, the Confederate infantry having approached to within a few hundred yards of the enemy without a break in their line, the enemy gave way and fled in disorder.

Several hundred prisoners were captured, and Sigel, crossing a bridge a few miles in his rear, burned it and made good his retreat nearly to the Potomac. The casualties to the Confederates were not as heavy as would be inferred from their exposed position, but among the cadets the loss was in proportion to their number the greatest, there having been seven killed and fifty-four wounded. It was a glory dearly bought, but gave to the corps a prestige which will endure for all time. No troops of veteran service ever bore themselves with more steadiness or valor or wore their honors with more becoming grace. General Breckinridge issued a special order commending them for their good behavior, and next day General Lee, relieved of the danger thus averted from his flank, sent to General Breckinridge his hearty congratulations.

On the same night, the rear of Lee's lines being threatened by a formidable raid of Sheridan, who had approached near Richmond, and at the Yellow Tavern had numbered among the dead the valiant and chivalrous J. E. B. Stuart, General Lee directed General Breckinridge to move as rapidly as possible to Hanover Junction and protect the bridges over the North Anna river. Accordingly, relieving the cadets, he started immediately for Staunton, and on the morning of May 20th arrived at Hanover Junction in time to save the bridges and protect the railroad. The celerity with which he had moved, and the thoroughness with which he had accomplished the purpose to which he was assigned, evoked the greatest applause throughout all Virginia. When, a few days later, the army of General Lee, falling back from Spottsylvania Court House, reached Hanover Junction, Breckinridge not only received in person the hearty thanks of that great commander, but whenever he came within the presence of the veterans of that grand army of Virginia, he was received with the most enthusiastic cheers, which rang down the lines until the sound faded out of hearing. They all knew what it meant and never tired in the ovation. And surely nature has rarely fashioned a man more calculated to inspire enthusiasm or evoke applause from his fellow men. Of a presence and manly bearing which even in the sober garb of a civilian would excite the admiration and attract the attention of the veriest stranger, in the uniform of an officer and superbly mounted as he always was, he was the very embodiment of manly grace coupled with intellectual force. Besides, his name was familiar as a household word to every man and woman of the South. After brilliant service in Congress from the home of Clay, whose mantle had descended with a blessing upon his shoulders, and whose eulogium he had fittingly pronounced in Congress, he had been chosen Vice-President at an age when he was barely eligible. Serving his term he had gone from the chair of the presiding officer to a seat for a full term in the Senate, after leading the forlorn hope as the choice of the Southern people for President. To these civic honors had succeeded a brilliant service in the army, where he proved his merit at Shiloh, Murfreesboro, Chickamauga, and other lesser battlefields. To few men has it been given to show such a record at the age of forty-three years—a period in life at only the threshold of mature and vigorous manhood. Nearly a quarter of a century has elapsed since he passed away, and yet there is no name in his native State which inspires more of genuine admiration for his superb manhood, or whose memory is more secure among her people, than that of John C. Breckinridge.

General Lee, by his masterly strategy, foiled General Grant, who, with his overwhelming numbers and great abilities as a general, was unable to get nearer to Richmond than Cold Harbor; whereon the 3d of June he was repulsed with a slaughter rarely equaled during the war, while the loss of the Confederates reached but a few hundred. General Breckinridge occupied an important position on the line of defense, and acquitted himself with his usual merit. He narrowly escaped death when his horse was killed under him by a solid cannon shot, and he was injured in the fall. In a few days after the battle he was again ordered with his division to the valley, to defend it against the advance of Gen. David Hunter. Of these operations it remains for other pens to write. Suffice it to say that for four months, in command of a corps under General Early, he fully sustained his reputation as an able officer. He was conspicuous at the battle of Monocacy in Maryland, July 9th, and a few days later saw the Capitol at Washington from the homestead of his relative, Francis P. Blair. At the battle of second Kernstown, July 26th, he executed a movement suggested by himself as the result of his habit of bold and thorough reconnoitering, which resulted in a decisive victory over a superior force, and which alone would have placed him in the front rank of military commanders. Not bred to the profession of arms, at a period when an education at West Point was regarded as a prerequisite for military success, he was undoubtedly the ablest general from the volunteer service, excelled by few who had the trademark of the profession, and superior to scores who claimed distinction by virtue of their diplomas rather than their merit or success in the field. After the battle of Winchester, Va., September, 1864, in which he rendered his usual service, he was ordered back to the command of his department, reaching there just in time to repel an attack upon the salt works, Gen. John S. Williams having opportunely arrived with a body of cavalry from Gen. J. E. Johnston's army and defeated Burbridge, who commanded the Federal force.

During the absence of General Breckinridge in the Shenandoah valley, General Morgan had made an extensive raid in Kentucky in June, doing much damage, but suffering severely at Mt. Sterling and Cynthiana. His command was much demoralized as the result of this expedition, and by the subsequent death of its distinguished chief.

In December, General Breckinridge successfully resisted a formidable raid against Saltville, led by General Gillem, who captured Wytheville, but was foiled in his further designs by the skill and energy of General Duke, under the personal direction of General Breckinridge. The cold weather was intense, and the men suffered much from exposure, but compelled the retreat of the enemy without any material results from the raid. General Breckinridge gave thorough satisfaction to the government as well as the people in the administration of his department. The citizens of Southwest Virginia found in him a commander who respected all their rights, and with the forces at his command, being chiefly Kentucky cavalry, protected them from the depredations of the enemy.

In the latter part of February, 1865, General Breckinridge was appointed secretary of war, and upon his acceptance his military career ended. He was succeeded by Gen. John Echols, a veteran officer of Stonewall Jackson's original brigade, afterward long identified with Kentucky in the development of her railroad system.

Upon the evacuation of Richmond by General Lee, General Echols marched with all his force eastward to join him. When near Christiansburg, he learned of the surrender at Appomattox. He called a council of war, and it was determined to furlough the infantry, indefinitely abandon the wagons and artillery, and march immediately with such cavalry as would go to General Johnston's army in North Carolina. General Duke and Gen. J. C. Vaughn elected to make the march, while General Giltner and General Cosby, regarding the war as practically over, concluded to march toward Kentucky and receive their paroles there if their conclusion was correct. Accordingly on the 12th of April, immediately after the council closed, the movement began. General Duke had about three hundred men, but they were not mounted, their horses being near Lincolnton, N. C., where forage could be obtained. His men were furnished with horses and mules from the abandoned wagons and artillery, and thus mounted, without saddles and with blind bridles, these men, together with Vaughn's brigade, accompanied General Echols two hundred miles to Salisbury. Here they met President Davis, who was much touched at the action of these Kentuckians, who had thus elected to share his fate.

General Echols in his report made to General Lee, after the surrender, says: "The bearing of General Duke's command, which with unbroken ranks faced the hardships of a march which was leading them at every step farther from home and to a destination full of danger and uncertainty was beyond praise. Even had they been fully equipped their bearing would have been worthy of praise, but when it is remembered that they were mounted on barebacked horses and mules with blind bridles, and nevertheless preserved the same discipline and order as upon a regular march, their conduct reflects great honor upon them." After a few more days they terminated their military service in the general surrender.

CHAPTER XIX

GENERAL JOHNSTON'S ARMY IN WINTER QUARTERS — GENERAL W. B. BATE SUCCEEDS GENERAL BRECKINRIDGE IN COMMAND OF DIVISION — OPENING OF THE CAMPAIGN — ROCKY FACE GAP — BATTLE OF RESACA — NEW HOPE CHURCH — ARDUOUS SERVICE OF THE KENTUCKY BRIGADE — CROSSING OF THE CHATTAHOOCHEE — GENERAL HOOD SUCCEEDS JOHNSTON — BATTLES AROUND ATLANTA — BATTLE OF JONESBORO — FALL OF ATLANTA — SEVERE LOSSES OF THE KENTUCKY BRIGADE — IT IS MOUNTED — ITS SERVICES IN THE SHERMAN CAMPAIGN AND FINAL SURRENDER AT WASHINGTON, GA. — OTHER KENTUCKY COMMANDS — DUKE'S AND BRECKINRIDGE'S BRIGADES — THE RETURN OF THE KENTUCKIANS TO THEIR HOMES — THEIR HOSPITABLE WELCOME — RESTORATION TO CITIZENSHIP — SPEEDY HEALING OF BREACHES

WHEN General Breckinridge was transferred from Dalton to Southwestern Virginia, he was succeeded in the command of his division by Gen. William B. Bate, of Tennessee, a gallant officer under whom the Kentucky brigade served during the campaign of 1864 with mutual satisfaction. Besides the Kentucky brigade the division comprised Tyler's Tennessee brigade and Finley's Florida brigade. The winter at Dalton passed quietly, the mountainous nature of the country between that place and Chattanooga rendering military movements impracticable. The winter quarters of the troops were comfortable, tents and rude huts built of small logs by the soldiers. The rations, however, were not always good or abundant, and contrasted unfavorably with those of the previous winter in Tennessee. The South was feeling the exhaustion caused by the war. The beef, chiefly from Florida, was of the leanest kind. Forage for the artillery and transportation stock was also difficult to procure. The health of the army, however, was good, its discipline well preserved, and the soldiers enjoyed many amusements in camp life, which experience had suggested.

General Sherman had succeeded Rosecrans in the command of the Federal army. The Confederate advance outpost was Ringgold, and in the latter part of February a demonstration was made against it, and the Kentucky brigade was moved to Rocky Face Gap, but their stay was of short duration, as the Federal forces soon retired. No further demonstrations were made of serious character until the first week in May, when the brigade was again sent to Rocky Face Gap and the long campaign of the ensuing summer may be said to have begun. On the 12th it fell back to Resaca, where on the 14th occurred the severest engagement which had to that time taken place. A large Federal force attacked the division in position, and the brunt of the fight fell upon the Kentucky brigade. After being twice heavily repulsed the attacking force withdrew, but shelled the slight defenses of the brigade with such effect that forty or more of the brigade were killed or wounded. By successive retreats and maneuvers for position, General Johnston fell back beyond Dallas, where, on the 25th, at New Hope Church, another stand was made, and an attack upon Hardee's corps by Hooker's corps was repulsed. On the 27th a part of the brigade was again engaged, and successfully charged the enemy's lines. But the heaviest engagement took place on the 28th, when the brigade made a notable charge, driving the enemy to his second line, in which the loss of both officers and men was heavy.

By continued flanking the enemy compelled General Johnston to continue his retrograde movement until, at Kenesaw Mountain, on the 27th day of June, another severe fight occurred in which the brigade sustained itself with its usual gallantry and with its usual losses. On the 9th of July General Johnston crossed the Chattahoochee river for the defense of Atlanta, but before there was another engagement he was superseded on the 19th by General Hood, a native of Kentucky, who at once assumed an aggressive policy. On the 22d, the enemy was attacked near Decatur, when the Kentucky brigade, under a terrific fire, lost in a few moments nearly one hundred and fifty men, the Federals being driven from their works and nearly one thousand prisoners and several pieces of artillery being captured. On the 5th of August a portion of the brigade was again engaged, and on the next day Gen. S. D. Lee, at this time commanding Hood's corps, to which the brigade temporarily was attached, issued a congratulatory order in which he said: "The lieutenant-general commanding takes pleasure in announcing to the officers and men of this corps, the splendid conduct of a portion of Bate's division, particularly Tyler's brigade [the Second and Fourth Kentucky regiments also participated], in sustaining and repulsing on yesterday three assaults of the enemy, in which his loss in killed, wounded and prisoners was from eight hundred to one thousand men, two colors, and three or four hundred small arms, and all of his entrenching tools. Our loss was from fifteen to twenty killed and wounded. Soldiers who fight with the coolness and determination that these men did will always be victorious over any reasonable number." Thus the command continued fighting from day to day in the entrenchments around Atlanta, and occasionally making sorties, until on the 29th of August they were sent to Jonesboro, to repel the advance of a heavy cavalry force, and there on the 1st of September, in addition to a number of killed and wounded, sustained the loss of about two hundred captured. Thus closed the long and arduous campaign of nearly four months, during which there had been no rest, since when not marching or fighting, these gallant soldiers had been exposed to the fire of artillery and musketry. The Atlanta campaign was at an end. The city was evacuated, and General Sherman's victorious army added to the destructive forces of the engines of war those of fire, until Atlanta was made the picture of desolation.

The brigade, what was left of it, was sent to Griffin, Ga., to be mounted in accordance with a long cherished wish. It was, however, but the skeleton of that robust body, small indeed, compared to its original roll before the ravages of Murfreesboro, Jackson and Chickamauga had depleted it, which had left its winter-quarters at Dalton in May. The history of the war shows no such record as that which attests the devotion of the Kentucky brigade. When the Georgia campaign began, it numbered eleven hundred men for duty, the remnant of that force which at Murfreesboro with its full complement of officers and artillery numbered five thousand. Now it mustered less than three hundred, the actual number of guns being two hundred and seventy-eight. Capt. Ed. Porter Thompson, in his history of the Kentucky brigade, page 262, says: "The loss during the campaign from Dalton to Jonesboro, it will be observed, had been eight hundred and forty-two non-commissioned officers and privates killed, wounded and prisoners, while the loss of officers was proportionately great. Only two hundred had been captured. One hundred and eighty rank and file had been killed, and at various times five hundred and thirty wounded, some of whom, however, had recovered and were now present. General Hardee reported the loss of the brigade to be greater than that of any other in the corps. For months there had scarcely been a day in which some were not killed or wounded, sometimes from forty to one hundred and fifty in a single day."

With the fall of Atlanta, besides the change in the service of the Kentucky brigade from infantry to cavalry, came also a new assignment in the line of service. It had up to this time always been attached to the army of the West, known first as the army of the Mississippi and then as the army of Tennessee. But now when General Hood with his army advanced north to attempt the capture of Nashville and to meet his Waterloo at Franklin, leaving Sherman to prosecute his "march to the sea," the brigade was detached from the army with which it had so long served, and left as part of the forlorn hope to impede Sherman's progress. The effect of the new order mounting the brigade was inspiriting to the men, as they had long desired the change, and it meant to them a relief from the drudgery of marching and the gratification of an inborn partiality of the Kentuckian for the horse. To the absentees of the brigade, the sick and wounded, and the men on detailed service, it acted as a healing balm for the first two, and brought applications from the last for return to active duty. So that when the brigade was mounted in October, with recruits from this source, and exchanged prisoners, it numbered about nine hundred men. They were mounted on such horses as could be procured, generally too poor for dashing cavalry, but available for transferring their riders from point to point and enabling them to do efficient duty as mounted infantry. There was practically no army with which to oppose the march of General Sherman except a weak corps of cavalry commanded by Gen. Joseph Wheeler, which served chiefly to hold in check the cavalry of the enemy and to protect the country from marauding expeditions. The brigade was placed in the division of Gen. Alfred Iverson, of Georgia, and served there to the close of the war, the division a part of the time being commanded by Gen. Pierce M. B. Young. The details of its operations were not of sufficient moment to follow minutely. It began its service on the picket line near Atlanta, and from the middle of November, when Sherman took up his march, its movements were retrograde for a month until Sherman captured Savannah. Then, when he turned northward, they followed over the ground made famous in the revolution by the cavalry of Sumter and Marion, but the conditions were not favorable for brilliant operations. In addition to the Kentucky brigade under General Lewis, Williams' brigade of cavalry, commanded by Col W. C. P. Breckinridge, served as part of General Wheeler's corps, being attached to the division of Gen. G. G. Dibrell. It comprised the First (Third) Kentucky cavalry, Lieut.-Col. Jacob W. Griffith; Second Kentucky (Woodward's), Maj. Thomas W. Lewis; and Ninth Kentucky cavalry, Colonel Breckinridge. In the Rebellion Records, Vol. XLVII, page 860, appears an order from General Hardee's headquarters, January 1, 1865, consolidating this brigade with General Lewis', but it was never carried into effect.

An inspection report of Maj. J. G. Devereux to Gen. Samuel Cooper, Richmond, dated February 10, 1865, gives the following account of the brigade: "The brigade commanded by Brig.-Gen. Joseph H. Lewis is composed of the Second, Fourth, Fifth, Sixth and Ninth Kentucky regiments of infantry, which were mounted both men and officers by command of General Hood, on public animals, mostly horses, but many of them mules, which have been receipted for by the acting quartermaster. The brigade lacks about 200 horses to complete its mounting. The men who need these horses are acting as infantry. The horse equipments are generally in good order and were mostly issued from government workshops. A detail of the men is making up the deficiency by constructing excellent saddles. It is gratifying to report that there are but few absentees without leave from this brigade."

Such was the condition of the brigade in the closing scenes of the war, and the picture applies as well to that of the other Kentucky troops. The end was near, and came at Washington, Ga., where, on the 6th of May, General Johnston having surrendered on the 26th of April, they received their paroles together with Breckinridge's brigade, and the remnant of General Morgan's command brought from Southwestern Virginia by General Duke, as heretofore detailed.

The Third, Seventh and Eighth Kentucky regiments, which at one time or another were associated with those of Lewis' brigade, received their paroles in the West. As has been stated, they were mounted quite a year before the Orphan brigade, and served with Forrest. One of their most notable fights was that at Paducah, March 25th, 1864, in which after a severe conflict, General Forrest was compelled to retire with serious loss. Here in sight of his home the gallant Col. A. P. Thompson, of the Third Kentucky, met his death, in the full tide of battle.

And thus the curtain fell upon the great drama which for four years held the eyes of the world, filled the soil of the South with the graves of her sons and of their opponents, and wrapped the whole country in woe and the South in desolation. To the Kentucky soldier the end brought sorrow equal to that of the more Southern States, since their hopes and affections had been as warmly enlisted in the cause for which they fought as those of any other State. At first it seemed that they would be denied even the privilege of returning home, as, although the right was granted in their paroles, the attorney-general at Washington, who was a Kentuckian, rendered an opinion that Kentucky, Maryland and Missouri not being within the Southern Confederacy, soldiers from those States had forfeited their homes and would not be permitted to return. After several weeks, however, this decision was rescinded, and gradually the weary and footsore found their way back to the paternal roof. The welcome which there awaited them went far to repay them for all the trials through which they had gone and to encourage them to gird their loins for a new struggle in the more peaceful pursuit of a livelihood.

The condition was changed from that which prevailed at the time of the Federal occupation, and during the war its scourge and the oppression of the satraps who had successfully exercised a despotic sway, had changed the whole current of political feeling. Men who had been prominent in handing over the State to Federal domination and had favored the hanging of so-called secessionists, had been sent to Northern prisons for protesting against the oppression of Burnside, Burbridge and Palmer, while Garrett Davis, who had succeeded Breckinridge in the Senate as a reward for his services in shackling the State, was as severe against the administration at Washington as his predecessor had been four years before, and was as roundly denounced as an arch-rebel. In fact the State was as ready for revolt under the leadership of those once most loyal as it had ever been under the State rights domination.

So that instead of coming home to be disciplined the Southern soldier was received with open arms as a hero by those from whom he least expected such welcome, and the parable of the prodigal son was exemplified. The fatted calf was killed and the veal was made his portion.

At the first election which followed in August, 1865, with soldiers at the polls and the returned Confederates disfranchised, the radical party was defeated, and two years later, upon a platform reaffirming the Kentucky resolutions, John L. Helm, an old-time whig, the nominee of the Democratic party, defeated his radical opponent for governor by a majority of over fifty-six thousand votes. Among the foremost to give welcome was the Federal soldier, who, having discharged his duty on the field of battle, was as generous to his late foe but now friend, as he had been brave. The next legislature repealed all disfranchising laws, and in time the ex-Confederates were rehabilitated and formed the conservative element in the anti-radical party. These facts in history must not be lost sight of, and should stand to the glory of Kentucky as much as the record of the military valor of her sons. Divided on the issues of the war, and with her sons confronting each other in the two armies, it is a matter of lasting congratulation that her internal wounds healed by the first intention and left no scars. There having been in the constitution of the State a clause which prohibited the giving or loaning its credit to any corporation or individual, no bonds could be issued as was done in many of the Southern States in the period of reconstruction, and hence there was nothing to attract the hordes of carpet-baggers and vultures who fattened on the plunder of less fortunate States, and Kentucky was left to adjust her own internal affairs without outside interference. In this way she escaped the terrors of reconstruction which befell the States farther South, and preserved her autonomy undisturbed, having peace within her borders, and enjoying a measure of prosperity in pleasant contrast with the misfortunes and hardships which befell the victims of the greed and vengeance of their oppressors.

CHAPTER XX

DIFFICULTY OF COMPILING MILITARY HISTORY OF KENTUCKY — MEAGER OFFICIAL STATISTICS — ORGANIZED COMMANDS IN CONFEDERATE SERVICE — APPROXIMATE NUMBER OF KENTUCKIANS IN FEDERAL AND CONFEDERATE SERVICE — LIST OF CONFEDERATE GENERALS FROM KENTUCKY — KENTUCKIANS AS SOLDIERS — THEIR PHYSIQUE AND RECORD FOR GALLANTRY — PROFESSOR SHALER'S ESTIMATE — THE KENTUCKY CONFEDERATES — THEIR HEAVY LOSSES — NUMBER OF BATTLES FOUGHT ON KENTUCKY SOIL — WORDS OF WISDOM FROM THE LEADER WHOSE DESTINIES WE FOLLOWED

IT has been a difficult task to write the military history of Kentucky from a Confederate standpoint. The facts that the enlistment and organization of the troops which served in the Confederate army were effected without State action, and that the muster-rolls have never been published, has made it impossible to write with that exactness attainable as to the organization and services of the various commands of other States, the history of which is preserved in the State archives. For much that has been written recourse has been had to the official correspondence and reports scattered through many volumes of the Rebellion Records, supplemented by the personal information of the writer acquired during the war.

In Washington are filed in confused mass the muster-rolls, captured among the Confederate archives, of the Kentucky troops which served in the Confederate army, but these are in no condition to furnish a complete or accurate history of the various commands, being full of palpable errors, both of commission and omission. Kentucky, of whose history their service is as much a part as that of the troops who served in the Federal army, should long since have had these records properly collated, edited and published, as she did with promptness in the case of the Federal commands. Sufficient time has elapsed to eliminate all partisan feeling, and the matter should not be deferred until those competent from possession of the necessary information for a correct execution of the work shall have passed away.

From these imperfect papers have been taken the following extracts, showing approximately the organizations, with the names of their commanders and the dates of commissions, now for the first time published:

First Regiment Kentucky infantry: Thomas H. Taylor, Colonel, October 14, 1861—Blanton Duncan, Lieutenant-Colonel, October 14, 1861—Thomas H. Taylor, Lieutenant-Colonel, July 3, 1861—Wm. Preston Johnston, Lieutenant-Colonel, October 14, 1861 — Edward Crossland, Lieutenant-Colonel, April 19, 1861—Benjamin Anderson, Major.

Second Regiment Kentucky infantry: James M. Hawes, Colonel, July 17, 1861—Roger W. Hanson, Colonel, 1861—Robert A. Johnson, Lieutenant-Colonel, July 17, 1861—James W. Hewitt, Major, July 17, 1861—James W. Moss, Major, Lieutenant-Colonel, Colonel—Philip Lee, Major, Lieutenant-Colonel, Colonel—Hervey McDowell, Major—Joel Higgins, Major.

Third Regiment Kentucky infantry: Lloyd Tilghman, Colonel, July 5, 1861—Albert P. Thompson, Colonel, October 25, 1861—G. A. C. Holt, Colonel, March 25, 1864 —Alfred Johnston, Major and Lieutenant-Colonel—James H. Bowman, Major—Al. McGoodwin, Major.

Fourth Regiment Kentucky infantry: Robert P. Trabue, Colonel, September 23, 1861—Andrew R. Hynes, Lieutenant-Colonel, September 23, 1861— Thomas B. Monroe, Major, September 23, 1861—Joseph P. Nuckols, Major, Lieutenant-Colonel, Colonel—Thomas W. Thompson, Major, Lieutenant-Colonel—John A. Adair, Lieutenant-Colonel—John B. Rogers, Major-Joseph H. Millett, Major.

Fifth Kentucky infantry: John S. Williams, Colonel, November 16, 1861—Andrew J. May, Colonel, May 21, 1861—Hiram Hawkins, Colonel, November 14, 1862— William Mynhier, Major, Lieutenant-Colonel—George W. Connor, Major, Lieutenant-Colonel — Richard Hawes, Major.

Sixth Regiment Kentucky infantry: Joseph H. Lewis, Colonel, November 1, 1861—Martin H. Cofer, Lieutenant-Colonel, November 1, 1861—William L. Clarke, Major and Lieutenant-Colonel—Thomas H. Hays, Major, October 8, 1861—George W. Maxon, Major.

Seventh Regiment Kentucky infantry: Charles Wickliffe, Colonel, November 1, 1861—Edward Crossland, Colonel, May 25, 1862—William D. Lannom, Lieutenant-Colonel—L. J. Sherrill,

Lieutenant-Colonel—H. S. Hale, Major, Lieutenant-Colonel—W. J. N. Welborn, Major.

Eighth Regiment Kentucky infantry: Henry C. Burnett, Colonel, November 11, 1861—H. B. Lyon, Colonel, February 13, 1862—A. R. Shacklett, Lieutenant-Colonel —Jabez Bingham, Major—R. W. Henry, Major.

Ninth Regiment Kentucky infantry: Thomas H. Hunt, Colonel, October 3, 1861—J. W. Caldwell, Lieutenant-Colonel, May 15, 1862, Colonel—J. C. Wickliffe, Major, May 15, 1862, Lieutenant-Colonel — Alexander Casseday, Lieutenant-Colonel—Ben Desha, Major.

Graves' Battery Kentucky artillery: Rice E. Graves, Captain, November 8, 1861; Major.

Lyon's and Cobb's Battery Kentucky artillery: H. B. Lyon, Captain, September 30, 1861—Robert L. Cobb, Captain, December 15, 1861; Major—Frank P. Gracey, Captain.

Corbett's Battery Kentucky artillery: C. C. Corbett.

Cumberland artillery, Kentucky: Henry D. Green, Captain—W. H. Hedden, Captain.

First Regiment Kentucky cavalry: Ben Hardin Helm, Colonel, October, 1861, first organization—J. Russell Butler, Colonel, September 2, 1862, second organization— J. W. Griffith, Lieutenant-Colonel—H. C. Leavill, Lieutenant-Colonel—Thomas G. Woodward, Lieutenant-Colonel—J. W. Caldwell, Major—N. R. Chambliss, Major.

Second Regiment Kentucky cavalry: John H. Morgan, Colonel—Basil W. Duke, Lieutenant-Colonel, Colonel— James W. Bowles, Major, Lieutenant-Colonel, Colonel— John B. Hutcheson, Lieutenant-Colonel—G. W. Morgan, Major—T. B. Webber, Major.

Third Regiment Kentucky cavalry (consolidated with First cavalry): J.Russell Butler, Colonel—Jack Allen, Lieutenant-Colonel—J. W. Griffith, Lieutenant-Colonel —J. Q. Chenoweth, Major.

Fourth Regiment Kentucky cavalry: Henry L. Giltner, Colonel, October 6, 1861—Moses T. Pryor, Lieutenant-Colonel—Nathan Parker, Major.

Fifth Regiment Kentucky cavalry: D. Howard Smith, Colonel, September 2, 1861—Preston Thompson, Lieutenant-Colonel, September 2, 1861—Churchill G. Campbell, Major—Thomas Y. Brent, Major, Lieutenant-Colonel.

Sixth Regiment Kentucky Cavalry: J. Warren Grigsby, Colonel, Sept. 2, 1862—Thomas W. Napier, Lieutenant-Colonel—William G. Bullitt, Major.

Seventh Regiment Kentucky cavalry: R. M. Gano, Colonel, September 2, 1862—J. M. Huffman, Lieutenant-Colonel—M. D. Logan, Major and Lieutenant-Colonel—Theophilus Steele, Major.

Eighth Regiment Kentucky cavalry: Roy S. Cluke, Colonel, September 10, 1862—Cicero Coleman, Lieutenant-Colonel—Robert S. Bullock, Major.

Ninth Regiment Kentucky cavalry: W. C. P. Breckinridge, Colonel, December 17, 1862—Robert G. Stoner, Lieutenant-Colonel—John P. Austin, Major.

Tenth Regiment Kentucky cavalry: Adam R. Johnson, Colonel, August 13, 1862—R. M. Martin, Colonel, June 1, 1863—G. Washington Owen, Major.

May's Battalion Kentucky and Virginia Mounted rifles (called also Tenth Kentucky cavalry): A. J. May, Colonel-George R. Diamond, Major, Lieutenant-Colonel—Edwin Trimble, Lieutenant-Colonel, Colonel — --------Cox, Major.

Eleventh Regiment Kentucky cavalry: D. W. Chenault, Colonel, September 10, 1862—Jos. T. Tucker, Colonel, July 4, 1863 — James B. McCreary, Major, Lieutenant-Colonel.

Twelfth Regiment Kentucky cavalry: W. W. Faulkner, Colonel, September 15, 1863—W. D. Lannom, Lieutenant-Colonel—John M. Malone, Major—Thomas S. Tate, Major.

Eleventh Regiment Kentucky infantry (known also as Thirteenth regiment): Benjamin E. Caudill, Colonel, November 2, 1862—David J. Caudill, Lieutenant-Colonel —Thomas J. Chenoweth, Major.

First Battalion Kentucky cavalry: Wm. E. Simms, Lieutenant-Colonel, 1861 — John Shawhan, Major and Lieutenant-Colonel.

Second Battalion Kentucky cavalry: Clar. J. Prentice.

First Battalion Kentucky mounted rifles: Benjamin F. Bradley, Major, 1861—Orville G. Cameron, Major, September 10, 1862, Lieutenant-Colonel.

First Special Battalion cavalry (Duke's Brigade, November 10, 1864): Wm. W. Ward, Colonel—R. A. Alston, Lieutenant-Colonel—J. G. Lowe, Major.

Second Battalion Kentucky mounted rifles: Thomas Johnson, Lieutenant-Colonel, March 12, 1862—Otis T. Tenny, Major.

Second Special Battalion cavalry (Duke's Brigade, 1864): Richard C. Morgan, Colonel—O. P. Hamilton, Lieutenant-Colonel—J. T. Cassell, Major.

Third Battalion Kentucky Mounted rifles: Ezekiel F. Clay, Lieutenant-Colonel, November 7, 1862 — Peter M. Everett, Major—John B. Holloway, Major.

Third Special Battalion cavalry (Duke's Brigade, November 10, 1864): Joseph T. Tucker, Colonel—T. W. Napier, Lieutenant-Colonel.

Company of Kentucky Scouts: Thomas Quirk, Captain, 1862.

Independent Company Kentucky cavalry: Bart W. Jenkins, Captain.

Jessee's Battalion cavalry (afterwards Sixth Battalion): George M. Jessee, Major.

Independent Company Kentucky cavalry: Thomas G. Woodward, Captain, August 25, 1862. (Afterwards known as Woodward's regiment: Woodward, Colonel — T. W. Lewis, Major)

Independent Company Kentucky cavalry: James M. Bolin, Captain, November 21, 1861.

King's Cavalry Battalion: H. Clay King, Major.

Independent Company Kentucky cavalry: J. J. Murphay, Captain.

Morehead's Partisan Rangers: J. C. Morehead, Colonel.

Patton's Partisan Rangers: Oliver A. Patton, Lieutenant-Colonel.

Buckner Guards (assigned to Gen. P. R. Cleburne's Division): Culvin P. Sanders, Captain.

Company of Kentucky Partisan Rangers: William J. Fields, Captain, August 1, 1862.

Company of Kentucky Partisan Rangers: Phil M. Victor, Captain.

There were other organizations composed in whole or in part of Kentuckians of which there is no official record; as Byrne's battery of artillery, which though first organized in Mississippi, was composed of and officered by Kentuckians almost exclusively, and won distinction in the service; besides many others less known. Kentucky contributed to the Confederate army a large number of able and distinguished officers, some of whom from their residence are credited to other States, but most of whom went directly from Kentucky. The following is the list with their rank:

General Albert Sidney Johnston (Texas.)

Lieutenant-General Simon Bolivar Buckner.

Lieutenant-General John B. Hood (Texas).

Lieutenant-General Richard Taylor (Louisiana).

Major-Generals John C. Breckinridge, George B. Crittenden, William Preston, Gustavus W. Smith.

Brigadier-Generals John. H. Morgan, Daniel W. Adams (Louisiana), Roger W. Hanson, Basil W. Duke, Abram Buford, Geo. B. Cosby, John S. Williams, James M. Hawes, Ben Hardin Helm, George B. Hodge, Claiborne F. Jackson (Missouri), Joseph H. Lewis, Samuel B. Maxey (Texas), H. B. Lyon, Randall L. Gibson (Louisiana), Thomas H. Taylor.

The number of the rank and file in the Confederate army can only be estimated, but the total number of officers and men of all arms is computed by those most competent to judge at 25,000, and represents strictly a volunteer force free from the call of any State or national authority or the offer of any bounty or contingent pension. Instead of such inducement the most of them went in the face of laws of expatriation, the virtual confiscation of their property, indefinite separation from their families, and with the fulmination of State and national wrath of the penalties of treason reserved for them. Rarely has such a spectacle been presented of men making such sacrifice for their convictions.

That there was similar heroism among those who espoused the Federal cause is readily admitted, but in their case there were many inducements besides those of mere principle, and this together with the protection afforded for enlistment, the influence of the presence of a friendly army, and the greater relative strength of the opposing governments, well accounts for the greater number who were enrolled in the Federal army. This has been estimated at 75,000 and includes not only those who threw themselves into the breach from principle, but also negroes, substitutes, drafted men, those secured by means of liberal bounties, and recruits drawn from the States immediately north, as in the First and Second infantry and the Third infantry, recruited largely in Ohio and Indiana and credited to Kentucky.

Whatever may be said of the character of the men whom Kentucky furnished to the Confederate army, the Federal statistics of the war show that judged by all the known physical tests, the Federal troops from Kentucky excelled those of all other States. In the history of Kentucky by Prof. N. S. Shaler, published in the Commonwealth Series, is exhibited, page 372, a table of measurements of American white men compiled from the report of the Sanitary Commission, made from measurements of the United States volunteers during the civil war, by B. A. Gould. In it is given the nativity of nearly one million men who served in the Federal armies, their height, weight, circumference of chest and head, and the proportion of tall men in each one thousand. An analysis of the table shows that Kentucky and Tennessee, which are grouped together, exceed in each particular those of every other State and foreign country, except that Scandinavia shows an excess of .05 of an inch in the circumference of the head. There was no such test made as to the physical properties of the Kentuckians in the Confederate service, but the testimony of Professor Shaler, a native Kentuckian, who was a gallant Federal soldier and who for more than a quarter of a century has filled the chair of Agassiz at Harvard university, as to the other merits of the Confederates from Kentucky, is well worth noting in this connection. Professor Shaler had noted the fact that Kentucky was peopled more directly by persons of pure English blood and had less proportion of foreign born population than any other State in the Union, the statistics of the eleventh census showing less than sixty thousand out of a total of nearly two millions. He then says on the subject under consideration:

"The rebel exiles who braved all consequences and forced their way through the lines to form Morgan's cavalry, the First brigade of infantry, the commands of Marshall and others, and the earliest volunteer Federal regiments, were probably the superior element of these Kentucky contributions to the war. They were the first runnings of the press, and naturally had the peculiar quality of their vintage more clearly marked than the later product, when the mass became more turgid with conscripts, substitutes and bounty volunteers. Had the measurements and classified results applied only to the representative native element, the standard of average of manhood would have been shown to be perceptibly higher. Though the ancestors of these soldiers had been fighting people, yet for forty years their children had known and followed only the peaceful pursuits of agriculture and the industries of trade peculiar to the commonwealth, with the limited exception of the Mexican war interlude, which made an inconsiderable draft of a few thousand volunteers during its brief existence. They may be said to have been wholly unused to the spirit and untutored in the arts of war. Yet their record of bold and daring skill, of heroic courage, and of indomitable endurance, was equal to that of the best troops on either side of the combatants in this great civil war, and certainly unsurpassed by the soldiers of Europe of the present or any past age. Take for illustration on the one side the force of Morgan, and we find in this remarkable body of men great capacity at once for dash and endurance. Its leader, suddenly improvised from the ranks of citizenship, not only organized, aligned and led this splendid squadron, but possessed the intuitive genius to develop a new feature in the art of war, in which was a rare combination of vigilance, daring fertility of resource, and an impetuous power of hurling all the husbanded force of body and mind into a period of ceaseless activity. Theirs was the capacity to break through the lines of the enemy, to live for weeks in an atmosphere of battle, fighting and destroying by day, and marching by night, deploying in front of the enemy or attacking his lines and posts far in the rear, a life that only men of the toughest and finest fiber can endure; yet this force owed its peculiar excellence as much to the qualities of the men and the subordinate officers as to the distinguished leader.

"Such a list of superior subordinate commanders as Basil Duke, Hynes, D. Howard Smith, Grigsby, Cluke, Alston, Steele, Gano, Castleman, Chenault, Brent, and others, was perhaps found in no other brigade of Kentucky cavalry. Yet at the head of their regiments and brigades such leaders as Woodford, Green Clay Smith, Hobson and others, showed qualities of a high order, and their commands proved to be the most effective cavalry of the war. The fighting of the Federal regiments of Kentucky infantry and cavalry throughout the great campaigns and battles of the war showed the men to be possessed of the highest soldierly qualities; but so merged were they in the great Union armies, and so little of distinctive Kentucky history has been collated or published of these, that we find it difficult to illustrate with the recount of their exceptional services."

Again at page 476, he says: " The most marked example of the character and success of the Kentucky troops in the Confederate infantry service has been given us in the well preserved history and statistics of the First Kentucky Confederate brigade. We have already noted the daring and gallantry of these troops in the battles of Donelson, of Shiloh, of Baton Rouge, of Chickamauga, and other conflicts, to Dalton, Ga., in May, 1864. On the authority of Gen. Fayette Hewitt, this brigade marched out of Dalton eleven hundred and forty strong on the 7th of May. The hospital reports show that up to September 1st, not quite four months, eighteen hundred and sixty wounds were taken by this command. This includes the killed, but many were struck several times in one engagement, in which case the wounds were counted as one. In two battles over 51 per cent of all were killed or wounded. During the time of this campaign there were no more than ten desertions. The campaign ended with two hundred and forty men able to do duty; less than fifty were without wounds. It will be remembered that this campaign was at a time when the hopes of the Confederate armies were well nigh gone, and they were fighting amid the darkness of despair."

Prof. Shaler adds that excluding the loss in the many smaller fights, between the home guards and other irregular troops and the raiding parties of the Confederates, "It is estimated that in the two regular armies the State lost approximately thirty-five thousand men by wounds in battle, and by disease in hospitals and elsewhere, contracted in battle. To these may be added several thousand whose lives were sacrificed in the State from irregular causes. There must be added to this sad reckoning of consequences the vast number of men who were shorn of their limbs, afflicted with internal disease bred by camp and march, or aged by swift expenditure of force that such war demands. Omitting many small encounters and irregular engagements in which there was much loss of life, but which have no place in our histories, Capt. L. R. Hawthorne in a manuscript summary of the history of the war enumerates one hundred and thirty-eight combats within the borders of Kentucky."

In conclusion, the writer, cherishing in vivid memory the deeds of the South in its struggle against great odds, yet with a feeling void of all bitterness toward those to whom it had to yield, and looking forward only to the future glory of a united republic, knows not how he can more fittingly close his work than in quoting the words of one whose pure life was sanctified by the sufferings he endured for his people, and who by fortitude under affliction wrung even from his enemies a tardy recognition of his exalted virtues. They are the closing lines of "The Rise and Fall of the Confederate States," by Jefferson Davis.

"The want of space has compelled me to omit a notice of many noble deeds both of heroic men and women. The roll of honor merely would fill more than the pages allotted to this work. To others who can say *cuncta quorum vidi,* I must leave the pleasant task of paying the tribute due to their associate patriots. In asserting the right of secession, it has not been my wish to incite to its exercise. I recognize the fact that the war showed it to be impracticable, but this did not prove it to be wrong; and now, that it may not be again tempted and that the Union may promote the general welfare, it is needful that the truth should be known, so that crimination and recrimination may forever cease, and then, as the basis of fraternity and faithful regard for the rights of the States, there may be written on the arch of the Union, 'Esto perpetua.'"

APPENDIX A

PROVISIONAL GOVERNMENT OF KENTUCKY

On the 18th of November, 1861, a sovereignty convention was held in Russellville, Kentucky, at which two hundred members were present, for the purpose of forming a State government favorable to a union with the Southern Confederacy. It remained in session three days and adopted a constitution which provided for a provisional government, vesting all executive and legislative powers in a council of ten, the council to fill vacancies. The existing constitution and laws were declared to be in force except where inconsistent with the acts of that convention and of the legislative council. George W. Johnson, of Scott county, was elected governor; Robert McKee, of Louisville, secretary of state, and Orlando P. Payne, assistant secretary of state; Theodore L. Burnett, of Spencer county, treasurer, who resigned December 17th, and J. B. Burnham, of Warren county, was appointed in his place; Richard Hawes, of Bourbon county, auditor, who resigned, and Joshua Pillsbury was appointed in his place. A. Frank Brown, of Bourbon county, was chosen clerk of the council; John B. Thompson, Jr., of Mercer county, sergeant-at-arms, and Walter N. Haldeman, of Louisville, State printer. An ordinance of secession was adopted, and Henry C. Burnett, William E. Simms and William Preston were sent as commissioners to Richmond, and on the 10th day of December, 1862, the Confederate Congress admitted Kentucky as a member of the Confederate States. Bowling Green was made the new seat of government. The following executive council was chosen: Willis B. Machen, president; John W. Crockett, Philip B. Thompson, James P. Bates, James S. Chrisman, Elijah Burnside, H. W. Bruce, E. M. Bruce, James M. Thorn, and Geo. B. Hodge, who resigned and was succeeded by Samuel S. Scott.

The following were elected representatives in the Provisional Congress from the several districts: First, Henry C. Burnett; Second, John Thomas; Third, Theodore L. Burnett; Fourth, Geo. W. Ewing; Fifth, Daniel P. White; Sixth, Thomas Johnson; Seventh, Samuel H. Ford; Eighth, Thomas B. Monroe, Sr; Ninth, John M. Elliott; Tenth, Geo. B. Hodge.

The council divided the State into twelve districts and provided for an election by the State at large of persons to represent these districts in the first permanent Congress of the Confederate States. On the designated day voting places were fixed and the election was held in all the counties within the lines of the Confederate army, resulting in the choice of the following: First district, Willis B. Machen; Second district, John W. Crockett; Third district, Henry E. Read; Fourth district, Geo. W. Ewing; Fifth district, James S. Chrisman; Sixth district, Theodore L. Burnett; Seventh district, H. W. Bruce; Eighth district, George B. Hodge; Ninth district. E. M. Bruce; Tenth district, James W. Moore; Eleventh district, Robert J. Breckinridge, Jr.; Twelfth district, John M. Elliott. These gentlemen served in the first regular Confederate Congress. Of the number, Messrs. Burnett, H. W. Bruce and Breckinridge survive, 1898. Mr. Machen was afterwards United States senator, 1873; John M. Elliott, judge of the court of appeals, 1878, and H. W. Bruce, circuit judge of the Louisville circuit court, 1868-73, and chancellor of the Louisville chancery court, 1874-80, while Geo. B. Hodge and Robert J. Breckinridge served as State senators, and James S. Chrisman as representative.

In 1863 the following were elected and sent as members of the second permanent Congress: First district, Willis B. Machen; Second district, Geo. W. Triplett; Third district, Henry E. Read; Fourth district, Geo. W. Ewing; Fifth district, Jas. S. Chrisman; Sixth district, Theodore L. Burnett; Seventh district, H. W. Bruce; Eighth district, Humphrey Marshall; Ninth district, E. M. Bruce; Tenth district, James W. Moore; Eleventh district, Ben. F Bradley; Twelfth district, John M. Elliott. Mr. Bradley afterwards served as State senator.

The legislative council, upon the admission of the State, elected Henry C. Burnett and William E. Simms senators to the Confederate Congress, and they served through the war. Upon the death of Gov. George W. Johnson, who fell on the second day at Shiloh, while fighting in the ranks, the legislative council elected Hon. Richard Hawes his successor. While the State was occupied by the Confederate army under General Bragg, Governor Hawes was inaugurated with due formality, and he delivered an inaugural address in the capitol at Frankfort, October 4, 1862, but the evacuation of the place the same afternoon prevented his performance of any of the functions of governor except the occupation of the executive mansion for a few hours. After the war he was county judge of Bourbon county for many years.

APPENDIX B

Gen. Albert Sidney Johnston's correspondence with President Davis in regard to his operations in Kentucky, his retreat from Bowling Green, the capture of Donelson, and the evacuation of Nashville, also as to his future purposes, is given here.

TELEGRAM TO PRESIDENT DAVIS.

Huntsville, March 7, 11 a.m.

Your dispatch is just received. I sent Colonel Liddell to Richmond on the 28th ult. with the official reports of Generals Floyd and Pillow of the events at Donelson, and suppose he must have arrived by this time. I also sent by him a dispatch containing my purposes for the defense of the valley of the Mississippi and for co-operating or uniting with General Beauregard, who has been urging me to come on.

The stores accumulated at Murfreesboro, the pork and provisions at Shelbyville and other points, and their necessary protection and removal, with the bad roads and inclement weather, have made the march slow and laborious and delayed my movements. The general condition of the troops is good and effective, though their health is impaired by the usual camp disorders and a winter campaign. The fall of Donelson disheartened some of the Tennessee troops and caused many deserters from some of the regiments, so that great care was required to inspire confidence. I now consider the tone of the troops restored, and that they are in good order. The enemy are about 25,000 strong at Nashville, with reinforcements arriving. My rear guard under General Hardee is protecting the removal of supplies from Shelbyville. Last evening his pickets were near Murfreesboro, but gave no information of an advance by the enemy. There are no indications of an immediate movement by the enemy from Nashville. I have no fears of a movement through Tennessee on Chattanooga. West Tennessee is menaced by heavy forces. My advance will be opposite Decatur on Sunday.

A. S. JOHNSTON.

To President Davis, Richmond.

LETTER FROM PRESIDENT DAVIS TO GENERAL JOHNSTON.

Richmond, Va., March 12, 1862.

My Dear General: The departure of Captain Wickliffe offers an opportunity, of which I avail myself, to write you an unofficial letter. We have suffered great anxiety because ot recent events in Kentucky and

Tennessee, and I have been not a little disturbed by the repetition of reflections upon yourself. I expected you to have made a full report of the events precedent and consequent to the fall of Fort Donelson. In the meantime I made for you such defense as friendship prompted and many years of acquaintance justified; but I needed facts to rebut the wholesale assertions made against you to cover others and to condemn my administration. The public, as you are aware, have no correct measure for military operations, and journals are very reckless in their statements.

Your force has been magnified and the movements of an army have been measured by the capacity for locomotion of an individual. The readiness of the people among whom you are operating to aid you in every method has been constantly asserted, the purpose of your army at Bowling Green wholly misunderstood, and the absence of an effective force at Nashville ignored. You have been held responsible for the fall of Donelson and the capture of Nashville. It is charged that no effort was made to save the stores at Nashville, and that the panic of the people was caused by the army. Such representations, with the sad forebodings naturally belonging to them, have been painful to me and injurious to us both; but, worse than this, they have undermined public confidence and damaged our cause. A full development of the truth is necessary for future success.

I respect the generosity which has kept you silent, but would impress upon you that the question is not personal but public in its nature; that you and I might be content to suffer, but neither of us can willingly permit detriment to the country. As soon as circumstances will permit, it is my purpose to visit the field of your present operations; not that I should expect to give you any aid in the discharge of your duties as commander, but with the hope that my position would enable me to effect something in bringing men to your standard. With a sufficient force, the audacity which the enemy exhibits would no doubt give you the opportunity to cut some of his lines of communication, to break up his plan of campaign, and, defeating some of his columns, to drive him from the soil as well of Tennessee as of Kentucky.

We are deficient in arms, wanting in discipline and inferior in numbers. Private arms must supply the first want; time and the presence of an enemy, with diligence on the part of the commanders, will remove the second, and public confidence will overcome the third. General Bragg brings you disciplined troops, and you will find in him the highest administrative capacity. Gen. E. K. Smith will soon have in East Tennessee a sufficient force to create a strong diversion in your favor; or, if his strength cannot be made available in that way, you will best know how to employ it otherwise. I suppose the Tennessee or Mississippi river will be the object of the enemy's next campaign, and I trust you will be able to concentrate a force which will defeat either attempt. The fleet which you will soon have on the Mississippi river, if the enemy's gunboats ascend the Tennessee, may enable you to strike an effective blow at Cairo; but to one so well informed and vigilant I will not assume to offer suggestions as to when and how the ends you seek may be attained. With confidence and regard of many years, I am Very truly your friend,

JEFFERSON DAVIS.

GENERAL JOHNSTON'S REPLY.

Decatur, Alabama, March 18, 1862.

My Dear General: I received the dispatches from Richmond, with your private letter by Captain Wickliffe, three days since, but the pressure of affairs and the necessity of getting my command across the Tennessee prevented me from sending an earlier reply.

I anticipated all you tell as to the censures which the fall of Fort Donelson drew upon me, and the attacks to which you might be subjected; but it was impossible for me to gather the facts for a detailed report or spare the time which was required to extricate the remainder of my troops and save the large accumulations of stores and provisions after that disheartening disaster.

I transmitted the reports of Generals Floyd and Pillow without examining or analyzing the facts, and scarcely with time to read them. When about to assume command of this department, the government charged me with the question of occupying Bowling Green, which involved not only military but political considerations. At the time of my arrival at Nashville, the action of the legislature of Kentucky had put an end to the latter by sanctioning the formation of camps menacing Tennessee, by assuming the cause of the government at Washington, and by abandoning the neutrality it professed; and in consequence of their action the occupation of Bowling Green became necessary as an act of self-defense, at least in the first step.

About the middle of September General Buckner advanced with a small force of 4,000 men, which was increased by the 15th of October to 12,000, and though accessions of force were received, continued at about the same strength until the end of November, measles, etc., keeping down the effective force. The enemy's force then was, as reported to the war department, 50,000, and an advance impossible. No enthusiasm as we imagined and hoped, but hostility, was manifested in Kentucky. Believing it to be of the greatest moment to protract the campaign, as the dearth of cotton might bring strength from abroad and discourage the North, and to gain time to strengthen myself by new troops from Tennessee and other States, I magnified my forces to the enemy, but made known my true strength to the department and the governors of States. The aid given was small. At length, when General Beauregard came out, in February, he expressed his surprise at the smallness of my force, and was impressed with the danger of my position. I admitted what was so manifest and laid before him my views for the future, in which he entirely concurred, and sent me a memorandum of our conference, a copy of which I send you. I determined to fight for Nashville at Donelson, and gave the best part of my army to do it, retaining only 14,000 men to cover my front, and giving 16,000 to defend Donelson. The force at Donelson is stated by General Pillow's report at much less, and I do not doubt the correctness of his statement; for the force at Bowling Green, which I supposed 14,000 effective men (the medical report showing a little over 500 sick in hospital),was diminished more than 5,000 by those unable to stand the fatigue of a march, and made my effective force on reaching Nashville less than 10,000 men. I inclose medical director's report. Had I wholly uncovered my front to defend Donelson, Buell would have known it and marched directly on Nashville. There were only ten small steamers on the Cumberland, in imperfect condition, only three of which were available at Nashville, while the transportation of the enemy was great. The evacuation of Bowling Green was imperatively necessary and was ordered before and executed while the battle was being fought at Donelson. I had made every disposition for the defense of the fort my means allowed; and the troops were among the best of my forces, and the generals, Floyd, Pillow and Buckner, were high in the opinion of officers and men for skill and courage, and among the best officers of my command. They were popular with the volunteers and all had seen much service. No reinforcements were asked.

I waited the event opposite Nashville. The result of the conflict each day was favorable. At midnight on the 15th I received the news of a glorious victory; at dawn of a defeat. My column was during the day and night of the 16th thrown over the river. A battery had been established below the city to secure the passage. Nashville was incapable of defense from its position and from the forces advancing from Bowling Green and up the Cumberland. A rear guard was left under Floyd to secure the stores and provisions, but did not completely effect the object. The people were terrified and some of the troops were discouraged. The discouragement was spreading, and I ordered the command to Murfreesboro, where I managed, by assembling Crittenden's division and the fugitives from Donelson, to collect an army able to offer battle. The weather was inclement, the floods excessive, and the bridges were washed away; but most of the stores and provisions were saved, and conveyed to new depots. This having been accomplished without serious loss, in conformity with my original design I marched southward and crossed the Tennessee at this point, so as to co-operate with Beauregard for the defense of the valley of Mississippi. The passage is almost completed, and the head of my column is already with General Bragg at Corinth. The movement was deemed too hazardous by the most experienced members of my staff, but the object warranted the risk. The difficulty of effecting a junction is not wholly overcome, but it approaches completion. Day after to-morrow, unless the enemy intercepts me, my force will be with Bragg and my army nearly 50,000 strong. This must be destroyed before the enemy can attain his object.

I have given you this sketch so that you may appreciate the embarrassments which surrounded me in my attempts to avert or remedy the disaster of Donelson before alluding to the conduct of the generals.

When the force was detached I was in hopes that such dispositions would be made as to enable the forces to defend the fort or withdraw without sacrificing the army. On the 14th I ordered General Floyd by telegram, "if he lost the fort, to get his troops back to Nashville." It is possible that this might have been done; but justice requires to look at events as they appeared at the time, and not alone by the light of subsequent information. All the facts in relation to the surrender will be transmitted to the secretary of war as soon as they can be collected in obedience to his order. It appears from the information received that General Buckner, being the junior officer, took the lead in advising the surrender and General Floyd acquiesced, and they all concurred in the belief that their force could not maintain the position. Subseqtient events show that the investment was not so complete as the information from their scouts had led them to believe. The council resulted in the surrender. The command was irregularly transferred and devolved on the junior general; but not apparently to avoid any just responsibility, or from any want of personal or moral intrepidity.

The blow was most disastrous and almost without remedy. I thereupon in my first report remained silent. This silence you were kind enough to attribute to my generosity. I will not lay claim to the motive to excuse my course. I observed silence, as it seemed to me the best way to serve the cause and the country. The facts were not fully known, discontent prevailed, and criticism or condemnation was more likely to augment than cure the evil. I refrained, knowing that heavy censures would fall upon me, but convinced that it was better to endure them for the present, and defer to a more propitious time an investigation of the conduct of the generals; for in the meantime their service was required and their influence was useful. For these reasons Generals Floyd and Pillow were assigned to duty, for I felt confidence in their gallantry, their energy, and their devotion to the Confederacy.

I have thus recurred to the motives by which I have been governed, from a deep personal sense of the friendship and confidence you have always shown me, and from the conviction that they have not been withdrawn from me in adversity. All the reports requisite for a full official investigation have been ordered

You mention that you intend to visit the field of operations here. I hope soon to see you, for your presence would encourage my troops, inspire the people, and augment the army. To me personally it would give the greatest gratification. Merely a soldier myself, and having no acquaintance with the statesmen or leaders of the South, I cannot touch springs familiar to you. Were you to assume command it would afford me the most unfeigned pleasure, and every energy would be exerted to help you to victory and the country to independence. Were you to decline, still your presence alone would be of inestimable advantage.

The enemy are now at Nashville, about 50,000 strong, advancing in this direction by Columbia. He has also forces, according to the report of General Bragg, landing at Pittsburg, from 25,000 to 50,000, and moving in the direction of Purdy.

This army corps moving to join Bragg is about 20,000 strong. Two brigades, Hindman's and Wood's, are, I suppose, at Corinth. One regiment of Hardee's division, Lieutenant-Colonel Patton commanding, is moving by cars today (20th March), and Statham's brigade, Crittenden's division. The brigade will halt at Iuka, the regiment at Burnsville. Cleburne's brigade, Hardee's division, except regiment at Burnsville, and Carroll's brigade, Crittenden's division, and Helm's cavalry at Tuscumbia; Bowen's brigade at Courtland; Breckinridge's brigade here; the regiments of cavalry of Adams and Wharton on the opposite bank of the river; Scott's Louisiana cavalry at Pulaski, sending forward supplies; Morgan's cavalry at Shelbyville, ordered on. Tomorrow Breckinridge's brigade will go to Corinth; then Bowen's. When these pass Tuscumbia and Iuka, transportation will be ready there to further other troops to follow immediately from these points, and if necessary from Burnsville. The cavalry will cross and move forward as soon as their trains can be passed over the railroad bridge. I have troubled you with these details, as I cannot possibly communicate them by telegram. The test of merit in my profession with the people is success. It is a hard rule, but I think it right. If I join this corps to the forces of Beauregard — I confess a hazardous experiment — those who are now declaiming against me will be without argument. Your friend,

A. S. JOHNSTON.

P. S. — I will prepare answers to the questions propounded by General Foote, chairman of the committee to investigate the causes of the loss of the forts, as soon as practicable; but engaged as I am in a most hazardous movement of a large force, even the most minute detail requiring my attention for its accomplishment, I cannot say when it will be forwarded to the secretary of war to be handed to him, if he thinks proper to do so.*

*This letter was begun on March 17th and finished March 20th.

GENERAL JOHNSTON'S ADDRESS TO THE ARMY JUST BEFORE SHILOH.

Headquarters Army of the Mississippi,

Corinth, Miss., April 3, 1862. Soldiers of the Army of the Mississippi:

I have put you in motion to offer battle to the invaders of your country. With the resolution and discipline and valor becoming men fighting, as you are, for all worth living or dying for, you can but march to a decisive victory over the agrarian mercenaries sent to subjugate you and to despoil you of your liberties, your property and your honor. Remember the precious stake involved; remember the dependence of your mothers, your wives, your sisters and your children, on the result; remember the fair, broad, abounding land, and the happy homes that would be desolated by your defeat. The eyes and the hopes of eight millions of people rest upon you. You are expected to show yourselves worthy of your lineage; worthy of the women of the South whose noble devotion in this war has never been exceeded in any time. With such incentives to brave deeds and with the trust that God is with us, your generals will lead you confidently to the combat, assured of success.

A. S. JOHNSTON, General Commanding.

The following epitaph was found shortly after the interment of General Johnston in St. Louis cemetery, New Orleans, pasted upon a rough board attached to his tomb:

IN MEMORIAM.

Behind this stone is laid, for a season,
Albert Sidney Johnston,
A General in the Army of the Confederate States, Who fell at Shiloh, Tennessee,
On the Sixth of April,
Eighteen Hundred and Sixty-two.
A man tried in many high offices
And critical Enterprises
And found faithful in all;
His life was one long Sacrifice of interest to Conscience;
And even that life, on a woeful Sabbath,
Did he yield as a Holocaust at his Country's need.
Not wholly understood was he while he lived;
But in his death his Greatness stands confessed

In a People's tears.
Resolute, moderate, clear of Envy, yet not wanting
In that finer Ambition which makes men great and pure;
In his Honor, impregnable;
In his Simplicity, sublime;
No country e'er had a truer Son—no cause a nobler Champion;
No People a bolder Defender—no Principle a purer Victim
Than the dead Soldier
Who sleeps here!
The Cause for which he perished is lost—
The People for whom he fought are crushed—
The Hopes in which he trusted are shattered—
The Flag he loved guides no more the charging lines;
But his Fame consigned to the keeping of that Time which
Happily, is not so much the Tomb of Virtue as its Shrine,
Shall, in the years to come, join modest Worth to Noble Ends.
In honor, now, our great Captain rests;
A bereaved People mourn him; Three Commonwealths
proudly claim him;
And History shall cherish him Among those choice Spirits
who, holding their Consciences unmixed
with blame,
Have been, in all conjunctures, true to themselves, their People
and
their God.

A

B

C

D

E

F

H

I

J

K

Q

R

S

T

U

V

W

CPSIA information can be obtained at www.ICGtesting.com
Printed in the USA
LVOW13s0836040813

346134LV00002B/479/A